_____

By

_____

On the Occasion of

_____

Date

_____

Jesus Is Here

Charles M. Sheldon

BARBOUR
PUBLISHING, INC.
Uhrichsville, Ohio

Published by Barbour Publishing, Inc., P. O. Box 719, Uhrichsville, Ohio 44683 http://www.barbourbooks.com

Printed in the United States of America.

INTRODUCTION

When you read *Jesus Is Here!*, remember that Charles Sheldon never intended his story to be taken either as prophecy or realistic fiction, any more than John Bunyan did when he wrote *The Pilgrim's Progress*. Like *The Pilgrim's Progress*, *Jesus Is Here!* is an allegory—it reveals spiritual truth symbolically, through fictional characters. The spiritual reality it reveals transcends the story's literal meaning.

We don't expect that Jesus will ever physically visit His church simply to comfort and console her. But although He is not present with us physically, Jesus *is* here. Sheldon reminds us of this truth in his sequel to *In His Steps.*

In the first novel, *In His Steps,* Sheldon challenged Christians to follow Jesus radically, absolutely. In the sequel, Sheldon issues another challenge that is just as radical and absolute: Don't just follow Jesus, but live in His presence!

Sometimes we are so accustomed to thinking of Jesus as Lord and King, that we set Him at a distance from ourselves. We forget He wants to share with us the ordinary, everyday moments of our lives. He wants to laugh with us, comfort us when we're tired, bless our human relationships, and walk with us daily, moment by moment.

Brother Lawrence, the author of *The Practice of the Presence of God,* was another Christian who advocated a real and intimate experience of Christ's presence. He wrote:

> *He is always near you and with you; don't leave Him alone. You would think it was rude to*

leave a friend alone who came to visit you—so why
do you neglect God? Then don't forget Him, but
think about Him often, adore Him continually,
live and die with Him; this is the Christian's glori-
ous business. In other words, it is our profession,
our vocation; if we don't know how to do it, then
we must learn.

Jesus *does* walk with us; He is truly present in our world today, though we are too often unaware of Him. And if our world is to see Him, too, then they must see Him in us. We are Christ's hands and mouth, feet and heart. Only through us can He fight for justice and dignity for those whom society abuses; only through us can He reach out with love and compassion to those who are suffering.

And in the world's suffering and downtrodden, we also find His presence. Remember what Jesus said? " 'For I was hungry, and you fed me. I was thirsty, and you gave me a drink. I was a stranger, and you invited me into your home. I was naked, and you gave me clothing. I was sick, and you cared for me. I was in prison, and you visited me'. . . . 'I assure you, when you did it to one of the least of these my brothers and sisters, you were doing it to me!' " (Matthew 25:35–36, 40, NLT).

Mother Teresa would have understood exactly what Charles Sheldon was saying in *Jesus Is Here!* In her book *The Love of Christ*, she wrote:

Let us put ourselves completely under the
power and influence of Jesus, so that He may

think with our minds, work with our hands, for we can do all things if His strength is with us.

Our mission is to convey the love of God, who is not a dead God but a living God. . . . Because we cannot see Christ, we cannot express our love to Him in person. But our neighbor we can see, and we can do for him or her what we would love to do for Jesus. . . .

In Sheldon's words:

"Jesus is here! Jesus is here!"
For is it not true, what He said:
"And lo! I am with you always, even unto the end of the world!"
And He does walk the streets of the world today. And our hearts have a right to cry aloud, as we do our work and bear our burdens:
"Jesus is here!"

PREFACE

The story *In His Steps* was written in 1896 and read one chapter at a time to my Sunday evening congregation. It was first published in the *Advance*, Chicago, in the fall of that year, and afterward published in book form in 1897.

The story *Jesus Is Here!* is supposed to begin seventeen years after the close of *In His Steps*. It continues the main characters of *In His Steps* with the addition of a few others. It was first published as a serial in the *Christian Herald*, beginning in 1913.

It has not been my purpose to describe what is called the "second coming" of Christ, but to picture another appearance of Jesus and describe His action in a modern world. The world today is far different from the world into which the historical Jesus was born. It is so different that entirely new problems relating to the human conduct face the modern Christian. It has seemed to me that it was a fair and reverent question to ask what would be the attitude of Jesus as He faced the complex conditions of modern society. It has also seemed to be a fair thing to try to bring back to our minds the great fact that Jesus was a very real everyday person. The lapse of time since He was here has removed Him in thought with very many people from the everyday life, and very many people have forgotten or at least do not remember that when He was on earth, He worked and ate and slept and grew tired just like any human being. He moved about among people just like any average man. He was not a recluse or a solitary, but He loved the multitude, and above all He was perfectly sympathetic with all sorts and conditions of people. No one ever lived who was more socially democratic than Jesus, and it is reverent to say no one enjoyed life more than He did.

I have received hundreds of letters from people, some of whom have severely condemned this story on the grounds that it is not reverent to bring Jesus into common human relations, that it takes away from His character as the redeemer of the world. Many of these letters declare the story to be blasphemous and have threatened the author if he ever dare publish the story in book form. On the other hand, the author wishes to express his appreciation of the hundreds of letters received from other people who have written him to express their thankfulness for the help that the story has given them in their Christian life. It is impossible for him to reply to all these letters individually. If any of the writers happen to see this, will they kindly take it as a reply on the author's part, thanking them for their kindness and expressing in part his appreciation of their understanding of his purpose in writing the story? The world needs to know Jesus as a real person, one who walks the earth and is a daily lover of us all; that is the main purpose of this story, to bring back to the thought of the modern world the living personality of the living Christ.

Charles M. Sheldon,
Topeka, Kansas, 1914

CHAPTER I

Fifteen years had gone by since the First Church in Raymond had adopted the motto "What Would Jesus Do?"

The pledge, as carried out by the members who had taken it, had revolutionized the church. Henry Maxwell still continued as the pastor. Many of the members of the church had been much disturbed by the rule Mr. Maxwell had introduced into the lives of the members, but a majority had sustained him, and he had continued to grow in the respect and affection of his large and growing congregation and in the respect of the businessmen and citizens of Raymond.

Mr. and Mrs. Maxwell were talking early one Friday evening about a gathering of old friends who were coming to the parsonage that night. It was the anniversary of the day when the First Church had taken the pledge to try to do as Jesus would do, and following a custom of several years, a dozen or more of the original company that had taken the pledge then were coming in after supper to talk over the old and new phases of their discipleship.

This evening Mr. Maxwell seemed strangely restless. He had gone over the list of those who were expected and had commented on different ones as his wife was asking questions. All the time he was talking, Mr. Maxwell paced back and forth between the large west window of the sitting room and the library, several times pausing to look with deepening and what seemed awed curiosity out of the window into the waning twilight.

"Will Rollin be able to come tonight?" Mrs. Maxwell had asked.

"I'm afraid not. He has been asked to go to Chicago and advise with the Commercial Club in regard to the social evil and take part in the eugenics congress. I think he planned to start this afternoon. But Rachel will come with Virginia."

"Doesn't it seem like a miracle to think of Rollin Page becoming an authority on these great social service questions?" Mrs. Maxwell said after another pause during which Mr. Maxwell had again stopped to gaze with a look of intense feeling through the big west window.

"It is a miracle. Mary, why should we take for granted that miracles are unnatural or uncommon? Or that they belong to any special age of the world? Why may we not expect miracles in our time? We need them. And Rollin is such a miracle. Nothing but a miraculous influence changed Rollin Page from a careless, selfish, worldly club man into a devout, earnest, religious lover of men, a new man all over himself, no more like the old Rollin than white is like black."

"Why, of course, if a change in a life like that is really a miracle, we have plenty of evidence that miracles still occur. But we don't generally call that a miracle, do we?"

"But what else can we call it? And did not the Master Himself say that His disciples would do even greater works than He Himself did? And do you know, Mary, I find myself of late longing, with a feeling I cannot express or explain, for a superhuman vision, for a real manifestation of the divine presence that somehow I cannot avoid feeling will be given to Christian disciples of this age. Oh, I long so for a real actual flesh and blood glimpse of Jesus. I feel at times as if I must see Him face to face. He said to His disciples, 'I am with you always, even to the end of the age.' If He is really in the world, why may we not see Him, really see Him sometime? I must see Him. My heart cries out for Him. I need Him. Not necessarily to strengthen my faith but to give Him in person some expression of my love for Him. And of late I keep wondering what Jesus would do and say in the world where we live. It is so different from the world in which He lived. I would give anything if I could see Him and hear Him and ask Him questions. And I have wondered so often of late—" Henry Maxwell paused and look over at his wife with deep thoughtfulness, "I've wondered if it might be possible somehow for Him to live on this earth again. It has been so long since He was here. And the world needs Him so much again. It has fought and sinned and suffered and loved and endured all through these centuries, doing wondrous things in His name and for His sake. Common people in one age of the world saw and felt and heard Jesus. Why should it not be possible for common people of another age to have the same glory shine around them? Why should not God give His Son to the world again and refresh its courage and strengthen its faith by a glimpse of Him who once came so long ago?"

She rose and came over to him. He had paused again in front of the big window and together husband and wife stood there, Mrs. Maxwell's hand on his arm, an anxious, troubled look on her face, wondering at the thought that seemed to be troubling her husband. But before she could speak, he had started forward and pointed eagerly out toward the farthest distance.

"There! It is out there again! That strange light! See! Mary! How it fills the sky! It cannot be twilight. It is too late. And we have seen it now for more than a month! What is it?"

Mrs. Maxwell could feel her husband tremble. She was more disturbed at the sight of his unusual agitation than she dared allow him to notice, and she answered quietly.

"We have spoken of it before, and you remember we agreed it might easily be caused by a number of reasons. You remember the peculiar light that flooded the sky several years ago when volcanic dust was wafted around the world from the earthquake disturbance in the Pacific islands?"

"But there is something about this wholly unlike all that. See! Mary! It is not an earthly light! It has a color and a radiance and a movement all its own. We have never in all our lives seen anything like it."

"You are unduly excited over it," said Mrs. Maxwell, again placing her hand soothingly on her husband's arm. "It cannot be anything but a natural light caused by some disturbance that we do not understand." But even as she spoke she could not resist an exclamation of wonder as she continued to gaze with her husband out through the window at what they both saw.

The softest, mellowest suffusion of pale blue swept up from the horizon and was met by what seemed an answering wave of deep crimson. And as the two waves mingled, the colors were softly blended into an unspeakably dissolving shade of pure white that could not be compared for one moment with sun or moon or star light. It pulsated like a wave backward and forward and filled not only the entire expanse of sky but seemed as well to fill up all inter-spaces of the firmament and fell over the earth like an immeasurable billow of radiance, the glittering spray from which was thrown up against the stars, and then subsided with a majestic slowness that spoke of all the world's accu-mulated forces somewhere lying latent and unspent, ready at any future time to repeat its glory for the pleasure of those who had the delicacy of spirit to understand it.

Henry Maxwell turned to his wife as the light softly disappeared.

"Mary, do you mean to tell me that such a light as that is caused by volcanic dust? Or earthquake distur-bance? It was the very glory of heaven. It was—what if it really was—the harbinger of His coming to earth again! What if—"

He was so excited and agitated that Mrs. Maxwell felt alarmed as she looked at him.

"It is not possible, Henry. You have allowed your imag-ination or your longing to get the better of your usual judgment. It is not like you to talk and act like this."

Mrs. Maxwell drew down the shade of the window and Mr. Maxwell made a strong effort to regain his usual calm manner as he walked back into the library and sat down.

"I expect you are right," he said with a sigh. "But it is a very unusual sight and I cannot account for it. I won-der the papers have not had more to say about it."

"Mr. Norman mentioned it in the *News* yesterday."

"True, he did. But the *Gazette* has not had a line. Mary—" Mr. Maxwell started up with a recurrence of his eager excitement as if a new thought suddenly possessed him. "Do you suppose—but no, it is all improbable. But we will ask Virginia and Rachel when they come. And Felicia. She and Stephen will be here. They are visiting Rachel this week. It will seem good to see them. And Alexander Powers and Dr. West. They must have seen the light! They must have seen it! And the Bishop—" Maxwell mused, talking to himself. "How I wish the Bishop were alive—I am sure he would have seen it. I am sure he would. I told them all to come early, Mary. And there is someone, now."

Answering a ring at the door, Mr. Maxwell went himself and ushered in Virginia, Rachel, and Felicia. The moment they came in, Mr. Maxwell noted the look of deep excitement on their faces.

Rachel was the first to speak.

"Have you seen it, Mr. Maxwell?"

"What?"

"The light!"

"The same that has been in the sky several times lately. The same—"

"But it was more wonderful tonight than ever before. We all noticed it on our way here."

"All of you?"

"Yes. We all saw it."

"Where is Stephen?"

"He is coming. He stopped to see Dr. West about the typhoid vaccinations at the Rectangle."

"What do you think of the light?" Mr. Maxwell

spoke to both Rachel and Virginia, after a pause.

The friends looked at each other very seriously, and Virginia said: "We have never seen anything like it in all our lives. There is something so unusual about it that we feel afraid. It seemed to us as we came here tonight as if we were being enveloped in fire."

"Yes!" Rachel broke in eagerly but with a low voice. "But did you notice, Virginia, that the people we passed did not seem to notice what seemed so strange to us?"

"How was that?" Mr. Maxwell leaned forward in his chair and spoke with a noticeable excitement of manner that Rachel and Virginia could not avoid remarking. "What was that?"

"Why, it seemed to us, to Virginia and me, as if we were enveloped in a most astonishing glory of light that must be felt by everyone, but we passed very many persons who did not seem to notice anything unusual."

"Only," Virginia broke in eagerly, "don't you remember, Rachel, once in a while some person would stop and exclaim and point up into the sky?"

"Yes, I remember that."

"Do you know who they were? I mean, the persons who noticed the light?" Mr. Maxwell asked, still leaning forward and speaking with excited interest.

"No, we couldn't see them, could we, Rachel?"

"I thought I heard Martha's voice," replied Rachel.

"Our Martha?" Mrs. Maxwell asked. "Probably it was. She just started a little while ago to the Rectangle church service. You know they have their meeting tonight instead of Thursday, and Martha is very faithful since she joined there."

"It was Martha, I am sure," said Virginia eagerly. "We passed her at the corner of Main and Third, and I remember I was going to stop and speak to her. Mrs. Maxwell, doesn't it seem like a miracle to think of Loreen's sister coming to us as she did, only one year after Loreen's death? And to think of Mr. Maxwell baptizing her on the day the Rectangle Church was dedicated. Every time I look at Martha I see Loreen. Poor Loreen!"

A tear fell from Virginia Page's eyes. Virginia had changed but little in seventeen years. She was still unmarried. Beautiful face and spirit, with no decrease of her old Christian enthusiasm as the years passed, she still lavished her wealth and her consecrated intelligence on the welfare of the people of Raymond. She had seen the Rectangle completely transformed since that day when Loreen had been struck down in front of the saloon where she had given her life in shielding Virginia, and through all the years that followed, Virginia had passionately and with deepest consecration devoted herself especially to the lives of women and girls in the city. Without a husband and children of her own, Virginia had nevertheless seemed to enter with complete understanding into the problems of the home life and needs of the women of Raymond, and she was known by them as the real source of great reforms in their social and industrial conditions. Rachel and Felicia would laughingly say that Virginia needed only a home of her own to be the most absolutely splendid and perfect woman of the world. Virginia would reply, her face deepening with fine color, that she was happy in helping to make other women have happy homes. It was the tragedy of women like Loreen that struck deepest into her heart, and when Mrs. Maxwell mentioned Martha, it brought up again the old vision of Loreen stumbling through the Rectangle that day. Virginia had brought the girl to her own home and caused her grandmother to leave the house in anger.

"To think of Martha a member of the Rectangle Church, Mrs. Maxwell! If Loreen could only have lived to see it! She told me while she was with me, after Grandmother went, about Martha and the fearful experiences she had gone through in the white slave traffic in Chicago. What a miracle! And what a joy to have her here with you of all women, Mrs. Maxwell!" Again Virginia's eyes filled as she impulsively laid her hand on Mrs. Maxwell's arm.

"You never saw a girl like Martha," Mrs. Maxwell replied with deep feeling. "The fearful things that girl suffered in Chicago are past belief. She endured unspeakable things. Twice she tried to kill herself, when she could not escape from the house where she had been imprisoned. But today she is the most devoted, faithful, enthusiastic disciple of Jesus you ever saw. I think I never saw a more complete love for Christ in any human being. And when it comes to loving her church, we all felt rebuked at the sight of her absolute passion for her church. Mr. Grey has taken full charge there, you know, and if he keeps on the way he has begun, it won't be long before the child of the First Church will outnumber in memberships its mother. Martha herself has brought at least twenty new members into the communion since she joined. And she is the most thoughtful, careful, helpful person about the kitchen I ever knew. All my 'hired girl' problems are solved since she came to me."

"Yes," said Mr. Maxwell, "all you need to do to get

Mrs. Maxwell started on the 'hired-girl problem' is to mention Martha. We haven't any troubles since she came into the house."

"It's true," Mrs. Maxwell eagerly assented. "That girl's religious enthusiasm shames me every day. She headed the subscriptions at the Rectangle with twenty-five dollars. We pay her all we can afford, five dollars a week, and she dedicates one-tenth of her income to church work. And she believes in Jesus just as if He were a real person living today and she might possibly meet Him around the corner any time."

"And isn't He living today?" murmured Mr. Maxwell. "But where? Where? And why shouldn't He live on the earth again—"

Rachel and Felicia and Virginia looked at him in astonishment, and Mrs. Maxwell again laid her hand on his arm as she had before when they stood in front of the window.

The bell rang and Mr. Maxwell, starting up as from a reverie, went to the door and admitted Dr. West and Alexander Powers and Stephen Clyde. The moment they entered the room they revealed in their faces the same serious look that had been borne by Rachel, Virginia, and Felicia.

They spoke almost together. "Have you seen it?"

"The light!" Mr. Maxwell exclaimed, and his voice was instantly echoed by the others.

"It has not been so beautiful nor so enveloping as this evening," said Alexander Powers.

During fifteen years Powers had experienced deep things in his heart and mind. From that night when the sound of Rachel's voice in the Rectangle had decided his course after the discovery of the Railway's breaking of law in the rebate cases, Alexander Powers had passed through a furnace of trial. Not for one moment had he turned back from following his Master. But his path had been rough and broken and his cross heavy. Yet the love light of the Redeemer shone steadily out of his great, patient eyes.

"You all saw it?" asked Maxwell, his old excitement rising again.

"Yes, all of us."

"It was astonishing." Dr. West spoke in a subdued voice but with the deepest feeling.

Stephen Clyde had walked over to Felicia. He and Felicia had a perfect married life. They would always be lovers. Stephen stood now by her while Felicia proudly noted her husband's handsome strength. Both had given themselves heart and soul to social service in the Master's name.

"Stephen," said Felicia gently, "what do you think of the light?"

"I don't know. There was something about it tonight that made me strangely both glad and fearful. It filled me with the deepest longing and at the same time my heart beat with something like terror."

"It had the same effect on me. Isn't it strange? What do you suppose—"

The bell rang again and Mr. Maxwell welcomed into the room President Marsh and Mr. Norman. The moment they came into the room their faces revealed the same excitement borne on the faces of the others who had come in before them. Edward Norman could hardly speak for emotion. He panted as if he had been running.

"Maxwell—this is a most astounding thing—this light—it is absolutely without a parallel. How do you account for it? Marsh and I—tried to explain it as we came along. It is not explainable."

"Unless—" Mr. Maxwell's face was deathly pale. His wife looked at him as she had all the evening with the same anxious, troubled look wondering at an unusual exhibition of feeling on her husband's part. "Unless, Norman, it might be—it might be—do you regard it as entirely out of the range of human events that Jesus might live among men again—"

"Henry!" Mr. Maxwell had come up to him as he stood in the middle of the room. The entire company was hushed into the most profound stillness. "Henry! What an impossibility! It is not—"

"But why? Why?" Mr. Maxwell persisted with a stubborn recurrence to the same thought, and yet he seemed timid about fully expressing it. "I don't know why if one age was permitted an actual sight of Jesus, another age—"

Mrs. Maxwell gently placed her hand on his arm and with a short laugh made him sit down by Mr. Norman. "I think, Mr. Norman," she said, talking directly to him while her husband unresistingly obeyed her motion, "I think Henry is rather nervous and not just like his usual calm self. He has been working beyond his strength for several months."

"I know he has, Mrs. Maxwell. It's going to be a fine thing for him to have the assistant the church voted last annual meeting. By the way, Maxwell, when does Stanton arrive?"

"Stanton? Oh, why, I had almost forgotten him. This light—Stanton wrote he might come in tonight. I told him to come right here as soon as he arrived, and he may come in any time. He wrote asking me not to trouble about meeting him at the station as he was not certain about the exact time of his arrival."

"I hope he will prove to be the man you need," said Mr. Norman.

"We believe he will," Mrs. Maxwell answered. "We used to know him when he was at the Settlement in Chicago. Mr. Maxwell feels confident no mistake has been made."

"About Stanton?" Mr. Maxwell spoke with great enthusiasm. "Stanton is a rare fellow. He is one out of ten thousand. First Church will never regret calling him, and he will be of the greatest possible help to me. He is forty years old, mature in his judgment, and a splendid fellow in every way."

"The only thing I have against him," Mrs. Maxwell said smiling, "is that he is not married."

As she said it, she happened to look toward Virginia, who was eagerly talking to Felicia and Stephen. Mrs. Maxwell seemed on the point of adding a word but did not. Mr. Maxwell simply said, "Oh well, Stanton will not cause any disturbance that way. He is the most confirmed single man I ever knew who was not at the same time disagreeably stubborn about it. He is passionately in love with the ministry. That is why I am so delighted to welcome him as my helper. And I shouldn't wonder if that was he."

The bell had rung as Mr. Maxwell spoke and he went hastily to open the door. The company gathered in the library could hear Mr. Maxwell's words of eager greeting and a very strong, deep voice replying, and the next moment Maxwell ushered in Richard Stanton, his new assistant, who received a very cordial welcome from all the members of the First Church who had anticipated his coming for several weeks.

Stanton was a big, healthy-looking man gifted with a rich voice and a most kindly smile, and most people felt friendly to him at sight. He exchanged greetings as he shook hands, and when he had completed the circle around which Mr. Maxwell had led him, he found himself by Virginia.

"Miss Page? Oh, I had the great pleasure of meeting your brother at the congress in Chicago. He made a splendid address at the opening."

Virginia was greatly pleased. "Rollin is splendid. We— I—am so proud of him."

Mr. Stanton was silent, but he seemed to be under some deep feeling, and as the others had begun to talk about various matters, he suddenly said to Virginia, "Miss Page, I had the most remarkable experience as I came along up here from the station. I sent my baggage up to the hotel, as Mr. Maxwell directed me to do if I reported here at the parsonage, and I walked up here. On the way a most astonishing gleam of light shot up across the sky and seemed to open and shut like a great white blossom. I wonder if you or any others have seen anything like it tonight."

Mr. Maxwell was near enough to hear a part of what Stanton said. He turned about eagerly, just as Virginia turned to him, and exclaimed: "Mr. Maxwell, Mr. Stanton says he saw the light as he came along. Can you describe it, Mr. Stanton?"

"No, I have never seen anything with which to compare it. I said it looked to me like a magnificent blossom spreading out the softest, whitest petals in a breadth and beauty I have never imagined possible. It was not like the aurora borealis, and I have seen that in its glory at the north, while with Missionary Landis at Hudson's Bay. I can't describe my feelings at the sight. I was awed and at the same time I was strangely excited. I have never had such a feeling in all my life."

Stanton's voice was remarkably deep, resonant, pleasantly penetrating; and without meaning to address anyone but Virginia and Maxwell, before he had finished speaking, every other person in the room had stopped talking and turned to listen.

Mr. Maxwell leaned forward and laid a trembling hand on his new assistant's arm.

"Did you notice other people and the effect of the light on them?"

"That was one of the most bewildering things about it to me. I was so excited by what I saw that I could not help exclaiming to a man I met, 'Isn't that great!'

" 'What?' he said, looking at me curiously.

" 'That light!' I said to him, pointing up at it.

"He looked up and replied, 'I don't see anything,' and passed along."

Virginia and Rachel and Felicia looked at one another. Stanton continued. "Have you people seen anything like this that I do not know how to describe?"

"We have all seen it," replied Mr. Maxwell. And at

that a silence fell over the company, a silence which no one seemed to wish to break.

Stanton looked gravely from one to another. The silence deepened. Out on the street the noises of the city could be heard, people passing on the sidewalk, the rumble of the street cars, the passing of carriages and automobiles. It seemed to the little company in the room that something out in the great world was portending, that they stood on the threshold of stupendous movements, but all undefined and shadowy, without a hint yet of what was to be, except as their troubled and excited hearts spoke of bewildering events such as had not occurred to mortals for centuries.

A door opened into the dining room. Someone walked, almost ran, through the room, and Martha stood at the library opening.

As long as life continues, no one in the group assembled there will ever forget the look on Martha's face.

She was a girl whose physical beauty had long ago been beaten out of her face by the bloody fist of brutal passion. But there had come to her after her redemption something infinitely more lovely than fleshly attraction. As she stood there in the opening between the curtains that parted the alcove, the look on her face was supreme in its glory, of unearthly pallor and superhuman exaltation.

She stepped into the room. Mr. Maxwell had faced her as he was nearest, and Martha said, not brokenly but clearly: "Jesus is here!"

"Here!" Mr. Maxwell spoke from lips that whispered.

"He is come to earth again! I have seen Him!"

No one in the room stirred or spoke. Martha stood,

her face glowing, her eyes fixed on Mr. Maxwell. No one knew how much time had passed when he said, with what sounded like unearthly calmness: "Where did you see Him, Martha?"

"At our church, tonight."

Again a silence, deep, uncounted, unmeasured. The little company took no account of time. Every eye was fixed on Martha. The girl seemed calm and at the same time there was that on her countenance that spoke of profoundest tumult.

"Yes, Jesus is here!" she repeated in a tone so low, with an ecstasy so thrilling that the group leaning forward in measureless excitement seemed to feel a tension break, and the next moment a tumult of questions might have poured about Martha, if Mr. Maxwell, his face white and a new look in his eyes, had not turned and said, "Wait! Let Martha speak. Tell us—what you—have— seen and heard—Martha."

Slowly, as if oppressed and almost stunned, but with clear and growing eagerness, Martha began to speak. But she had not said more than a few sentences before everyone was crowding up near her, asking questions, pleading for answers, bewildering her with their demands to know —and yet not one of them caught even the faintest glimmer, not even Mr. Maxwell, of the stupendous events that were to follow Martha's story, nor could they grasp the astounding fact even in the faintest degree that they were about to enter upon a succession of great experiences that would create new history for humanity and make the heart of the world beat as it had not throbbed for nearly two thousand years.

SOMETHING TO THINK ABOUT

1. Why do you think not everyone can see the strange light in the sky?

2. Everyone who sees the light feels "both glad and fearful." How would *you* feel if you saw some sign of Christ's actual presence?

3. Although we often fail to see Him, Christ *is* actually present in our world today. What are the signs in our world of His presence?

CHAPTER II

The torrent of questions that the assembled company poured upon Martha bewildered and confused her. She stood near the place where she had stopped when she entered the library and looked appealingly at Mr. Maxwell.

"I can't answer all these questions at once," she said slowly. "Mr. Maxwell, I maybe can't answer some of them at all. You ask me, one at a time. Perhaps I can tell something."

The girl was trembling with intense excitement, and Mr. Maxwell, who was the calmest person in the room now, noticed it and said: "Sit down, Martha. We will all be seated. If what Martha says is true—it does not seem possible but—"

He put his hands over his face and tried to control his growing agitation. By an effort he succeeded in calming himself and as if by common consent, after a moment of silence that seemed all the more strange following that sudden outburst of eager questions, the company was still, while Mr. Maxwell put their questions to Martha.

The girl sat now with her hands folded, her eyes looking at Mr. Maxwell with deep seriousness and a quiet assurance in her answers that caused her eager listeners greater feeling than the noisiest assertions.

"What happened first?"

"He appeared right in the middle of our meeting and spoke to us."

"How did He appear? What did He look like?"

"I didn't notice Him come in. He just was there."

"What did He look like?"

Martha was naturally a slow girl in her speech. Mrs. Maxwell sometimes said it was her one fault. In reality it was not a fault; it was simply a habit that went with her phlegmatic character. She seemed, however, to the intensely eager listeners around her to be unusually slow in answering this question.

"I don't believe I can tell."

"You can't tell how He looked! But you saw Him and you are sure He was Jesus?"

"I only know He looked"—Martha spoke with painful slowness—"He looked just like a common man, and at the same time different."

"What did He say?" Mr. Maxwell asked, thinking best to come back to the other question later.

"He comforted us," said Martha so simply that a deep silence followed.

"But what did He say?"

"He said how glad He was to know about our church, and He praised all the good it was doing. And He mentioned the First Church and spoke your name, Mr. Maxwell, and a lot of other names in First Church, Mrs. Maxwell, and Mrs. Page, and Mrs. Clyde and Mr. Clyde, and Miss Virginia and the new assistant, Mr.—Mr.—"

"Stanton," said Mr. Maxwell, while his eyes glowed.

"Yes, Mr. Stanton. He seemed to know all of you. And Mr. Norman and Mr. Powers. He said beautiful words about all of you. He didn't blame the church for anything. Just praised its great work."

There was another period of silence in the library while Martha sat looking wistfully at Mr. Maxwell.

"And what else?"

"What else did He do? What else did He say?"

"That was about all."

"And you can't tell us how He looked?"

"No, sir. Not very well. I don't think I thought of it."

"But how do you know the person you saw was Jesus? Did He do any miracles?"

"Miracles?"

"Yes. Wonderful works. How did He try to prove He was Jesus? How do you know it?"

Over Martha's face an astonishing look passed. It was reminiscent of her troubled life before she came to Mrs. Maxwell's. And then she said very slowly: "After the meeting, Jesus spoke to me and told me things about my life in Chicago ten years ago. And He mentioned Loreen. He said He knew her."

Virginia broke out with a cry as she stretched her hands toward Martha. "He mentioned Loreen!"

"He did, Miss Page. And He said she was happy where she was."

Again that tense silence fell over the company, smitten into awed stillness by Martha's simple but tremendous statement.

"But some stranger might have found out the facts about you and Loreen. How do you know—"

"But no stranger could tell me about things that no one but myself ever knew. Mr. Maxwell, He told me in a few words all about my real sinful life—things I have never told, not even to Mrs. Maxwell."

"And you feel sure He—this person—was really—Jesus?"

"I know it."

"How did the rest feel? What impression did this person make on the other people at the meeting?"

"They all felt as I did. Mr. Maxwell, when you see Him, you will feel just as I did. You cannot doubt. No one can doubt."

Again a period of silence. The whole thing was so stupendous if it were true that their hearts and minds could not grasp it and their very speech was smitten into silence.

"Where is He—this person—now? Where did He go after the meeting?"

"He went home with Mr. Grey."

"He is with Mr. Grey now?"

"I suppose so. Mr. Grey invited Him to come with him and they went away together."

Edward Norman's old reportorial instincts came to the front. "Call up Grey over the phone and ask him—"

"Yes, I'll do that in a minute," Mr. Maxwell said. "But I want to ask Martha a few more questions. Can't you tell us, Martha, how He looked?"

"No, I don't believe I can, Mr. Maxwell. He looked to me just like an average man, only different."

" 'An average man, only different,' " murmured Stanton, and even his low tone was deep and penetrating. "Why should He look any other? Why should we expect to see a face like those painted by stereotyped art, when we know well enough there is no authentic

32

portrait of Jesus in existence?"

"That is what the world will expect to see," said Virginia. "It has had a certain type of face presented by art for so long that it will expect to see some such countenance as that painted by the old masters."

"It is all incomprehensible to me," said Maxwell. "But what does all that mean if Jesus is here? That is the main thing after all. Martha—" He turned again toward her, as if he felt there must be something she had held back without meaning to conceal any real facts. "Martha, did this person say who He was? Did He call Himself Jesus?"

Martha leaned forward eagerly. "Yes. He said two or three times like this— 'I am Jesus! I have come to visit the earth again. I have come to comfort My disciples and help on My Kingdom!' Like that! And it all seemed so good. Oh, I cannot express it."

Again, as so many times that evening, a deep silence settled over the little company, trying to measure something immeasurable.

"And did He say anything about the length of His stay or His plans?"

"No, I don't remember that He did."

"Did He say anything to the people in the meeting about not making Him known?"

"Not that I heard. He talked as freely and openly as anyone could."

"What was the one thing that impressed you most about Him, Martha?"

"I think it was His great joy and His air of victory."

Again the silence stole over all the little company. Mr. Maxwell broke it by turning to Mr. Norman. "Edward," he said, using Norman's first name as he had been doing for several years. "I'll call up Grey and you question Martha about anything else you have in mind that I have forgotten."

He went over to the telephone, which was in the hallway, and called up the pastor of the Rectangle Church.

Mr. Norman did not try to ask Martha any questions, and as if with one consent, everyone was listening to the one-sided talk over the telephone.

"Yes. I'm glad to hear your voice, Grey. We've just been talking with Martha, our girl here, you know—She—

"Of course we can't believe it. You say what—

"You really believe it—yourself—

"Asleep? Now? At your house—

"Can you come over—Norman is here—and Rachel and Virginia, and the regular company, and Stanton has come in—

"In about half an hour—all right. We can hardly wait to see you."

Mr. Maxwell hung up the receiver and came back into the library. The profound seriousness of his face had deepened.

"Grey says he has no doubt whatever. I had hardly spoken his name before he said, 'Jesus is here!' Actually in his own house, asleep there. Can we comprehend that?"

"Only," said Stanton, whom everyone was fast beginning to like for his fine combination of poet and man of action, "only, of course, when He was here before, He slept in common people's houses and wore common clothes and ate common food and was a practical carpenter. Why should we expect anything different now

34

He has come again?"

"Do you accept it as a fact that He has actually come again?" Mr. Maxwell put the question as if he were afraid Stanton would say no.

"I would be as willing to take Martha's evidence as quickly as anyone's. Can anyone say it is impossible for Jesus to live on the earth again?"

"Not impossible but improbable," said Stephen Clyde.

"And why improbable? Has it not seemed to all of us in the last ten years as if the whole world was on the very eve of tremendous happenings in the church, and in the social, business, and commercial, and political life of the people? Why, it has been almost like a spoken word of God every day. I do not find myself stunned at the thought of Jesus being here. Somehow it does not seem unnatural. It seems opportune. He is needed here now."

"I have had the same feeling," Mr. Maxwell spoke eagerly. "I have not been able to shut my mind to the vision of His possible coming. The need is so great. But the thought of His being here in actual person terrifies me. What will He say? What will He do? What judgment will He pass on the church and the ministry?"

"Martha said He did not say a word of censure. It was all praise of the church. Didn't you say so, Martha?" asked Mr. Maxwell.

"He comforted us." Martha repeated like a child her former statement. "After He was through talking, I never felt so proud of being a church member. It seemed to me He mentioned every good thing we had ever done and told us how it gladdened His heart."

"Didn't He say anything about the hypocrites in the church?" Powers asked.

"He did not condemn anyone. He spoke every word in the spirit of love."

"And you can't tell us how He looked?" Mr. Maxwell persisted.

"No, Mr. Maxwell, I really can't. Have you never met people you could not describe?"

Mr. Maxwell could not help smiling at Martha's earnestness. The company continued to ask her questions, going over the entire scene in the mission church again while waiting for Mr. Grey.

At last they heard his step on the porch, and Mr. Maxwell opened the door before he could ring the bell, and Grey came into the library. The minute he appeared, his face revealed the tremendous experience through which he was passing.

Mr. Grey had begun his career as a professional evangelist. He had been of the quiet persuasive type, not sensational at all in his methods, and above all, a man of deep and sincere spiritual earnestness who had one purpose, to bring souls to God through Christ. He had been very successful as an evangelist in work at the Rectangle, and when the mission there, started by his converts, had developed into a church, the people had clamored for him as their pastor. He had accordingly taken charge of the church and with the help of Mr. Maxwell and the First Church, he was rapidly shaping a strong and very useful body of disciples, most of whom had been, like Martha, among the social outcasts of the city. One phrase may describe Mr. Grey in his personality: He was absolutely consecrated to religious work. His one passion in life was to save souls. Mr. Maxwell often said Grey was the most unselfish and Christlike man he ever knew.

The first words he spoke were the same as those uttered by Martha, "Jesus is here!"

Again, that silence. Through the strange weeks that were to follow, how often that same awe-inspiring silence was destined to fall over the disciples of Jesus in many places and under many different circumstances. It seemed to be a part of the entire history of His appearance. The noisy earth had been full of clangor and uproar so many centuries. When had the people kept still to think of God? Their very definition of religion had been bustle, activity, energy, talking in meeting. Were these silences now to reveal that quiet approach to the Divine that is so necessary before one can approach the real needs of the world?

Grey went on in a natural, deeply happy tone: "He appeared in our meeting tonight. The moment He rose and spoke I knew it was He. My heart and my mind together welcomed Him. Oh, it is the most wonderful thing! But it is actually come to pass! Jesus is here!"

"He is with you?" Maxwell asked in a whisper.

"He is in my house, asleep."

"Your guest?"

"My guest. In my home."

"What does He look like?" Three voices asked the question at the same time.

"Like an average man—only—different."

"There! I told you the same!" cried Martha.

"But that does not describe Him," said Mr. Maxwell.

"Why not?" It was Stanton speaking. "What are we

37

to look for? An angel? Would He not appear as an average man, yet different?"

Grey looked around on the eager, excited group.

"What Mr. Stanton says is true. When you come to see Him, you will understand how impossible it will be for you to describe His appearance in literal terms. And yet no one of you will for a moment doubt that it is Jesus. Jesus is here! On the earth again! I have seen Him! He has spoken in our church! He is a living presence in the flesh among us!"

"What will all this mean?" Mr. Maxwell again spoke almost inaudibly.

"It will mean everything for the church!" Grey spoke with intense earnestness. "The church is under fire. It is being criticized. It is being scorned. Did you not all read that editorial in the *Gazette* only two nights ago advising the closing of all the churches in Raymond on the ground that they were useless and an unnecessary expense?* And even our religious papers are full of articles deploring the weaknesses and shortcomings of churches and church members, speaking of the church as a weak and inefficient organization, whereas in reality it is the most powerful and useful institution in the world today."

Within the six months since the writing of Sheldon's story a number of such editorials had appeared in daily papers in this country, actually advocating closing all the churches in the towns where these papers are published.

"Just as Mr. Norman wrote in his reply in the *News*," said Virginia.

"But the ministers and church members never needed so much as right now to be assured of that fact. And the coming of Jesus will be the greatest impulse the church ever had to begin an entirely new and wonderful chapter of its history. Oh, if you could have heard Jesus speak to our people tonight! He declared the church to be the most useful and necessary of all institutions and said His own disciples did not understand its mighty power and greatness."

"Grey, do you actually believe this person is Jesus? The same Jesus whom the world crucified twenty centuries ago?"

"I am as certain of it as I am certain I am here with you. No one can question His identity."

"But what is your proof? What is the real proof that people are going to accept?"

"Just Himself. He is His own proof. No one can deny Him. Some will not see anything but a common man at first, but I believe there will be times when all the people, His own disciples and others, will be compelled to bow down to Him as King of Kings."

"Do you think He will do any miracles to prove His personality?"

"No, not to prove it. But I believe He can do them if it is necessary for any purpose. The whole bearing of the man breathes power of an infinite quantity."

"Martha says He told her things about her life that no one but herself could possibly know."

Grey's face filled with intensest interest. "Yes, He spoke to her after the meeting. It seemed to me He spoke to everyone in the room personally. And on the way home tonight, He said things to me that simply astounded me

39

because they revealed such an intimate knowledge of my own history and feelings."

Again, that silence. . . No one seemed to count the time. It passed by unnoticed, unthought of. Then Mr. Maxwell was saying: "Do you suppose—He—this person—you are so sure is Jesus—would preach for us next Sunday? What are His plans? What will He do? What is His purpose? It is all too bewildering to entertain. We will not know how to approach Him."

"Approach Him!" Grey exclaimed, while his eyes flashed with an indescribable exultation. "He is the most approachable person I ever met. There is not a particle of pride or aloofness about Him. He is the most companionable person I ever met."

"Why not? Is not that what we ought to expect in Jesus?" Stanton's deep voice spoke. "Would He be Jesus if He were not the most companionable person Grey or any of us ever met?"

"The whole thing is beyond belief!" Maxwell cried out. "I have been longing for this very thing for years. Now that it has come, if it has—I feel unable to comprehend it."

"Don't try to comprehend it, Mr. Maxwell. Just enjoy it," said Martha, who sometimes revealed a depth of thought that made Mr. Maxwell wonder in what school she had learned it.

"Then we can see Him at your house in the morning?" Maxwell turned to Grey as all the others had done.

"Yes. There is one thing He said definitely. He will visit churches and His disciples everywhere. How long He may stay in Raymond I don't know. But that is His purpose at first. He has come to comfort and encourage His own."

Everyone was too much wrought up over the great event of the evening to feel sleepy, but Grey finally went home, and Stanton went along to his hotel. Rachel, Virginia, Dr. West, and Felicia and Stephen soon went away. Alexander Powers and Norman stayed a little longer. Norman was especially excited, as a newspaperman, over all the future possibilities of events from the standpoint of an editor and journalist.

"Maxwell," he said, talking in his regular steady manner but with a deep undercurrent of excitement, "if all this unparalleled thing is true, it opens up a most tremendous field for thought. I feel simply aghast when I try to imagine what will happen."

Henry Maxwell was very thoughtful. His first excitement had given way to a profound seriousness. Finally he said: "Edward, don't you think we can leave all that to Him? Do you doubt He will know what to do under all circumstances, just as He did—before?"

Norman actually stared at Maxwell. Then he said with a sigh of relief, "I confess I had not thought of it in that way. I was only thinking of our own newspaper vulgarity and the hasty, superficial treatment of every serious thing. I don't know how it will all come out. But of course I don't doubt His own wisdom and ability to face any situation of modern life. Can you make yourself believe that such a marvelous event has really occurred—that Jesus Christ in the flesh—is actually living and breathing in Raymond tonight?"

"I believe it without question." Alexander Powers

41

spoke softly, almost as if talking to himself. Throughout the evening, he had sat silent, only occasionally uttering a word, deeply absorbed in Martha's answers, observant of all shades of expression, and tense with suppressed feeling. To anyone who was familiar with this man's history and the cross he had borne in loyalty to his Lord, it might have been revealed that night that Powers was in a state of exaltation, free from any particle of hesitation or doubt. He had accepted, with a heart that was hungry for a look at its Lord, the entire stupendous statement of Martha from the moment she had exclaimed, "Jesus is here!" and henceforth his entire faith would rest calmly and joyfully on this person and call him Master and Lord.

Not so Mr. Maxwell. He confessed to Norman and Powers and Mrs. Maxwell and Martha as they remained in the library after the others had gone that he could not yet bring his mind to accept such an astounding event as a real fact. In spite of his own intense desire for such an appearance and in spite of all Martha and Mr. Grey had said, he found a region of doubt still existing in his own heart. He found himself murmuring almost mechanically, "Except I shall see in His hands the print of the nails, and put my hand into His side, I will not believe."

"I accept it wholly!" Alexander Powers's voice broke through Maxwell's reverie. "I believe He is here. I don't doubt my Lord and my God. What an unheard of joy to see Him at last!"

Tears rained over Alexander Powers's face. His friends understood it. When he and Norman went away, Maxwell said, "Powers, I want to believe as much as you do. And I have a feeling that I shall as soon as I meet—Him. I am going over to Grey's the first thing in the morning. Did I tell you, the last thing Grey said to me tonight was that—He—the person—had told him He wanted to see me early tomorrow."

Mr. Maxwell did not sleep that night. And he welcomed the early light. As soon as the simple morning meal was over, he went out. Mrs. Maxwell laid her hand on his arm as he left the house, simply saying, "It will be all right, Henry. Leave it with the Father."

The town looked just the same as always. At that early hour people were still going to work. Maxwell did not take the *Gazette*, which was an evening paper, but as he passed down through the shop district adjoining the Rectangle, he heard a newsboy crying out something about "great story—Rectangle church meeting—last night! Special edition!"

He refused to buy a copy thrust at him by another boy as he turned the corner into the street where Grey lived. But when he came up to the house, he noticed a number of young men, two with cameras, standing outside and recognized them as *Gazette* reporters.

He walked up to the door and rang the bell. The reporters crowded about him. Grey opened the door. One of the newspaper boys tried to force his way in. Grey politely but firmly blocked his entrance.

"Come in, Mr. Maxwell, we have been waiting for you," he said quietly. He did not even reply to the general clamor of the press representatives to be allowed to get in. As soon as Mr. Maxwell was in the hall, Grey locked the door, then turned, looked at Maxwell with a look of deepest feeling, waited a moment, and then ushered him into the sitting room. Mr. Maxwell's heart beat with tremendous excitement as he entered the room and saw the person waiting to receive him.

SOMETHING TO THINK ABOUT

1. When Jesus was on earth two thousand years ago, He worked signs and miracles to prove to people who He was. Today we seldom see miracles—and yet, as Sheldon reminds us in this chapter, Christ's absolute power is undiminished. Why do you think miracles are so rare today?

2. Why do you think the people who see Jesus in this story can only describe Him as "average" and yet "different"?

3. Some of the believers in Raymond accept Jesus' presence easily, while others, equally committed Christians, cannot help but doubt. In our world today, do you ever find it hard to believe that Christ is actually present? Why or why not?

CHAPTER III

M r. Jasper Carter, editor and proprietor of the *Raymond Evening Gazette*, appeared very much annoyed over something that had occurred in the office. It was the morning after the astonishing scene at the Rectangle Church and about two hours after Mr. Maxwell had been admitted to Mr. Grey's house.

Mr. Carter was often annoyed at many things in the course of a day's work at the *Gazette* office and his temper was often at the exploding point. But this morning he was even more than usually irritable and out of sorts.

Nothing was going right anywhere. He had succeeded in getting a "scoop" on the *News*, Mr. Norman's paper, by getting an exceptional early extra describing the meeting at the Rectangle and putting into the "story" all the dramatic touches of which Barnes, his best reporter on the staff, was capable. Barnes had not been present at the meeting, but he wrote a full account of it as if he had been and even went so far as to describe the appearance of this "visitant from another world." And there were three columns of interviews, garbled and distorted, with members of Grey's church, some of whom had not been present at the meeting. Altogether the "story" made intensely interesting reading to many families in Raymond that morning before they started on their day's work.

But Mr. Jasper Carter was thoroughly dissatisfied. For

some unaccountable reason he had not succeeded in getting any reliable information concerning this mysterious person who claimed to be Jesus. Not even the indefatigable if irrepressible Barnes had secured anything really tangible. And now for some unaccountable reason there was no report from either Barnes or the new cub reporter who had been sent out to secure a picture of the newcomer at all costs. He had sent the "cub" because, as he grimly said, "Sometimes these absolutely green hands can get what the old seasoned newspaper veterans can't get. They have a reputation to earn instead of sustain and a man will do more impossible feats to earn fame than to keep it up."

The particular "cub" reporter assigned with the veteran Barnes to do this particular work was a young man by the name of Logan. He had claimed to be an expert photographer and Barnes had hired him as an experiment for a week, thinking he looked unusually ambitious.

Another hour slipped by and Mr. Carter simply boiled over. He jerked the telephone receiver off the hook and called up Grey's number. But although he savagely called to central to keep ringing, he received no answer and was just throwing the receiver back when the new reporter came running in.

The look on the boy's face stopped even Carter's oath at the sight of him. As a general thing no reporter old or young would have rushed into Carter's office in this fashion, but Carter saw in a second that something tremendous, at least to the boy, had occurred. He held the negative of a photographic plate in his hand and after an ineffectual stammer, he exclaimed:

"Mr. Carter—look—at that! I climbed into the kitchen

through a window at Grey's and got up on a table and opened a transom and got a time exposure of the man you wanted. He was talking with Mr. Grey and the other man, Mr. Maxwell. I ran all the way back here and have just come from the developing room. And I ask you to look at that!"

Carter took the bit of glass and held it up to the light. It was perfectly clear, not a shadow of any sort visible on it.

"Well, what of that—you—" Carter swore. "Something wrong with your plate, or your developing, or your focus. Go out again and don't come back till you get what I sent you for!"

"There was nothing wrong with the plate, the focus, or the developing," Logan replied doggedly.

"No! That's right! The only thing wrong is your stupid self. Do you mean to tell me—"

"Mr. Carter!" the boy broke in, out of eagerness more than in a spirit of resentment at Carter's manner. "I can't understand it. Everything was as right as it could be. I have been using the same plates right along. And—"

But Jasper Carter was beside himself. He fairly roared at Logan. "Get out! And if you can't come back with what I want, don't come back at all!"

He fairly drove Logan out of the office and slammed the door shut. This door usually stood open on the hall that connected all the other editorial, reportorial, and telegraph editors' rooms. But Carter was so enraged at what he considered the cub reporter's stupidity that he did not want to see anyone for a while, and so when he heard the door open and Barnes came in, he turned savagely.

"Oh, it's you! Well?"

"Look here, Mr. Carter! Call me a fool if you want to! But look here!" He held up a photographic plate still wet. It was clear and without a shadow.

"I waited outside Grey's for him and Maxwell and—" Barnes paused curiously, while over his hard features an inscrutable glance moved and disappeared—"and the other person, and just as they stepped out, I got a good shot. He was looking squarely at me. And—you can think what you like, but—here is all I got!"

"Let me see!" Carter's hand shot out with a vicious gesture, and in the attempt to pass the plate over to him, it slipped out of Barnes's fingers and fell on the floor, breaking into small pieces. Barnes stooped down and picked up one of the larger fragments and held it up to the light, looking at it as if fascinated.

"This will make the greatest 'story' yet, Mr. Carter. It's great."

"Oh get out! Do you mean to tell me—" Carter spoke roughly.

"I mean to say I had as fair a shot as I ever had at anyone and there is the result."

"You and cub Logan must have a nice bunch of plates," and Carter in a few words retailed the incident of Logan's failure to secure a negative. Barnes listened gravely and did not reply to Carter's sarcastic advice to overhaul the developer.

He sat thoughtfully eyeing the editor and did not reply to a question until Carter had angrily asked it twice.

"Can't you tell what He looked like?"

"Yes. He looked like an average man—only different."

"How? Different?"

"I can't describe it exactly. But He was different."

"Well, go on," Carter said impatiently when Barnes stopped, while the same shadow of wonder crossed his face as when he was looking at the photographic plate.

"When He came out of Grey's house with Grey and Mr. Maxwell, I was as near Him as I am to you now. He stopped and spoke naturally and pleasantly to all the newspapermen and answered questions. He is going to preach in Maxwell's church tomorrow. I forgot to say He has a most wonderful voice. I have never heard anything like it anywhere."

"Well," said Carter. "What then?"

"He walked along with Mr. Grey and the Reverend Maxwell and—" Again that pause—so different from Barnes's usual self-satisfied, jaunty manner, as if his eyes and his thoughts were intent on something far different from the surroundings in Carter's office.

"Well, what's the matter with you?" Carter's sharp voice broke in.

"As He went up the street toward Mr. Maxwell's house, a number of schoolchildren came down the walk. We were all following along, and two of the children broke from the group they were with, went right up to—this—person—" Barnes uttered the word with strange hesitation— "and each child took a hand—and turned and walked along with Him. Mr. Maxwell called them by name and said they belonged to his Sunday school. But they didn't come to him, they came to this stranger."

"Well, what of it?" said Carter gruffly.

Barnes looked at the editor silently, then answered: "Nothing."

"Nothing?"

"Yes. That's what I said. Nothing."

"The whole affair is nothing so far. What have we got from all this fuss and mystery. Can you turn out two or three columns for the edition?"

"I think I can," Barnes replied, but Carter detected a strange note of hesitation.

"What's the matter with you?" he asked angrily.

"I don't know, Mr. Carter. I feel very queer after seeing—Him. I don't know how to describe it. You will know better after you have met Him."

"Well, maybe I shall. But look here, Barnes. Of course we will play up the story about this mysterious stranger who calls Himself Jesus as long as it makes good for the *Gazette*, but don't expect me to be gulled by any faker or any mysteries beyond clairvoyance or hypnotism or the like. Don't tell me that in this age of the world anything supernatural is possible in Raymond. Oh no! You can't deceive your Uncle Jasper with any such romance."

"Wait till you see Him," Barnes said, still speaking with that unusual backward mental glance over the morning's incidents.

"Well, I will see Him. I'll go to church tomorrow. I don't know when I've been," he added with a short laugh. "Guess it won't hurt me."

"You'll have to go early to get in. Word is getting all over town. Everybody is going."

"Can't you get Maxwell to reserve us seats? I hate to go too early and wait."

"I don't think there will be any reserved seats," Barnes answered briefly. "Mr. Maxwell said the doors would be open at eight o'clock."

"Eight o'clock! Do you think I am going at that hour to wait until eleven?"

"You'll have to if you want to get in," said Barnes, as he went out of the office.

Carter called after him sharply, "Overhaul your camera and the whole outfit. It's simply nonsense to come off as you did this morning. I have already sent that cub up to Maxwell's to get a picture. He needn't come back unless he gets it!"

"You sent—" Barnes began, and then closed his lips and walked down the hall to the reporters' room.

He clicked off his "story" on the typewriter with characteristic rapidity, but it outran his notes and he had piled up a three-column article before noon. He took it down to the first edition linotype man and then went out on the street.

A large crowd was in front of the *Gazette* office eagerly reading the *Gazette* bulletin announcing in brief lines the afternoon edition. Several of Barnes's acquaintances excitedly stopped him to ask questions. He put them all off, referring them all to the paper that was then running off the press. In less than half an hour the boys were out on the streets crying out the news. It was a significant fact that they had caught the one line at the head of Barnes's "story" and were shouting it carelessly. Barnes had at first written it with a question mark at the end, like this, "Jesus is here?" while back in his mind the question represented a sarcastic sneer that everyone who knew him would understand perfectly well. But as he had pounded out his "story" up there in the reporters' room, as he drew near the end and read over what he had written, he crossed out the question mark and wrote for the heading, "Jesus is here!" with an exclamation point after the three words.

And this was what the boys were calling out on the streets. Before the night of that memorable Saturday, the words were being uttered in nearly every home of the city. Businessmen gathered in groups on the corners, discussing the unheard-of event. A crowd surrounded Mr. Maxwell's house, watching every window and door. People called one another up over their telephones and excitedly talked the matter over. The members of Grey's church who like Martha had been present at the meeting Friday night were sought out and eagerly interviewed. And the whole town was moved as if by a common thrill of expectation.

In the midst of all the excitement, it was curious to note the contradictions and rumors that were affirmed and denied. He was of such and such an appearance. He was of no special significance. He had said this. He had not said it. The whole thing was an imposture. It was real. Men like Mr. Maxwell and Mr. Norman, it was said, believed Him to be Jesus. And so forth.

That night in Raymond was calm and starlit. Virginia and Rachel were together at Virginia's, and during dinner they had been talking as thousands of people all over Raymond were talking about the one great event. Rachel was staying with Virginia while Rollin was in Chicago.

Virginia went over to the west window of the familiar library to draw down a shade and stopped abruptly. Then she called to Rachel, who was in the sitting room with her two children, Eloise and Frank. The children had come with Rachel to feel that Virginia's home was like their own, and they called her aunt.

"Come quick, Rachel! Come! The light!"

Rachel caught up both children and ran in; setting the boy down on the broad window seat and letting the girl slip to the floor at her feet, she sank into a convenient chair.

Together the two friends watched in silence. The evening star was visible just above the tower of the First Church, which was only four blocks from Virginia's home on the boulevard. And at first Rachel saw nothing beyond the regular beauty of the star. But as she looked, Virginia exclaimed again: "There! There! Don't you see it? There! Just below the star!"

It was entrancing in its unearthly radiance, inde-scribable in its soft yet penetrating color—that which fell out of the blue vault like palpitating winds, as if the angelic host were singing, an unnumbered company, beating the air with a glory that permeated space and included in its all-enveloping wonder all the planets in addition to earth. Never had light been so diffused, so liv-ing. It had a personal charm as if at any moment a Face might appear, smiling but grand, to give body and a name to that which seemed almost to speak. And while they looked and even listened as if a voice might speak, the radiance gently went out, and there hung the star as it had for centuries, now calmly shining over the black roofs of Raymond.

Virginia turned to Rachel. She was trembling and tears were on her face.

"Oh, it is so wonderful, I cannot control myself.

53

How terribly beautiful! Can you comprehend it, Rachel?"

"No. But how can we comprehend what has come to Raymond within the last twenty-four hours? It does not seem possible. Do you realize, Virginia, that tomorrow, in the church where we promised only a few years ago to follow Jesus, we shall actually see Him face to face?"

"I cannot believe it. I can hardly wait. And yet I dread it. What if all this should be an imposture. What if—"

"But why, Virginia? Why should it be impossible? Think what it will mean to Raymond and to the world. For of course we cannot expect Him to stay here very long. But I tremble to think what His reception will be in some places."

"But will He not be welcomed by His disciples, Rachel?"

Rachel spoke with deep feeling. "Oh surely He will. The church loves Him. Is it not glorious, Virginia, to think He has chosen to show Himself first of all to His church? And how splendid that on the very Sunday when Mr. Stanton was to be recognized as Mr. Maxwell's assistant, Jesus should be with us. Isn't that splendid?"

"Yes," Virginia answered in a low tone. "It is as it should be."

Silence fell between the two friends as Rachel moved to the window seat and cuddled the children in her lap. After a while she spoke again.

"What do you think of Mr. Stanton, Virginia?"

"He seems—well—different from most men. Not what I had expected."

"What had you expected?"

"I hardly know. More of a ministerial type."

"What is a ministerial type, Virginia?"

Virginia did not answer directly. "He wore a gray suit, a sack coat, and a brown silk tie."

"Otherwise," said Rachel teasingly, "he was dressed in perfect taste. Virginia," and her manner changed instantly to a deep seriousness, "did you notice how he—Jesus—was dressed?"

"Like the others. I did not give it a thought."

Rachel, cuddling her children, crooned a little night song and looking down at the happy sleeping faces said, "About bedtime, childers."

But it was so serene there in the old library where Virginia and she had in the past gone over so much together that was so great in their Christian experience, that Rachel lingered and went on to speak again of the wonderful tomorrow.

"We shall have to go early to get in. They say everybody will be there."

"I long for it, and at the same time I dread it," Virginia said. "I cannot bear the thought of some things that may happen. The vulgar curiosity, the impertinence, the newspaper accounts, the—"

"But," Rachel interrupted gently, "He endured things like that when He was here before and He always silenced His enemies. Do you believe He will fail in our age of the world? The people are the same now as then."

"Yes, the people. The common people are always the same. But how about the rulers—the financiers—the proud and exclusive, the so-called great—how will they treat Him?"

"The same as they did before, no doubt," Rachel said

sadly. "But you must remember, Virginia, how many more good people there are now than then. Think of the church people. Think of the missionaries and Christian workers all over the world who will welcome Him. Before, He came to His own, and His own received Him not. Can you imagine that His own disciples, thousands of them, will not receive Him today?"

"No. I cannot believe that. No. His church will welcome Him. And did not Martha say again and again that when He spoke to them last night He had only words of comfort and praise for the church?"

"That was one of the first reasons why I began to believe in Him. He has come to cheer His own disciples, to enlarge their definition of themselves, and declare to them the power they possess. Not to denounce and criticize but to inspire and encourage."

There was another silence. Then Rachel said: "I have been thinking of Mr. Stanton also and rejoicing in the fact that Mr. Maxwell is to have such a fine assistant. Did you notice what a splendid voice he has?"

"Yes."

"Most men have common voices, Virginia. Of course Rollin is an exception." Rachel laughed happily.

"Rachel," Virginia spoke wistfully, looking at her as she sat there in all her motherly beauty, folding her children in her arms, "your married life has been a joy to you, hasn't it?"

"It has been heaven to me."

"Those children—how much they mean to you—"

"I believe I should die if anything should happen to the darlings. Eloise has not been real well today. But

56

nothing serious."

Another silence was broken this time by Virginia.

"Mr. Stanton seemed to me to be something of a mystic as well as a man of affairs."

"Do you object to that?"

"Oh no. I rather like that combination in a man. It makes an interesting person."

"I hope he will be as interesting a preacher as he is a talker. Sometimes a man with a good voice like his loses it when he begins to preach."

"I don't believe he will. And oh, let us hope he will not 'holler.' Let us hope that, won't we, Virginia?"

"By all means. If he 'hollers,' I shall not go to church. Mr. Maxwell has set us all a high example that way." Virginia laughed.

The bell rang, and a moment after, the maid announced, "Mr. Stanton to see Mrs. Page."

"Mrs. Page?" Virginia had risen.

"Yes, he said Mr. Maxwell told him Mrs. Page was here while her husband was in Chicago and he has stepped in with a message from Mr. Maxwell to her."

Rachel rose and put the children on the couch.

"We will both go," she said to Virginia. And taking her hand, she drew her into the hall reception room where Stanton was standing. He sat down at Rachel's invitation and said he would remain only a few moments.

"Mr. Maxwell is very anxious to have you sing tomorrow, Mrs. Page. I know you have told him you are out of practice and all that and that you had expected to be absent in Chicago tomorrow. But now you are here, he feels that no one can sing as you can and he wants you tomorrow especially. That is my errand. I hope you will sing?"

During the years of her married life Rachel had gradually dropped her music, and since much of her time had been spent in Chicago, where of late Rollin had been so much engaged, she had given up her place in the choir of First Church. But her voice had still the charm of the old days and she loved to sing to her friends.

She said instantly, "Tell Mr. Maxwell I will sing and do my best."

"Thank you," Stanton said simply. Then he added as if it were the most natural thing in the world: "I have just come from Mr. Maxwell's and—I—have seen Jesus."

Again that silence—that pause—that the world was going to note so wonderfully in its feverish life.

"There is no doubt about it. Mr. Maxwell met Him at Mr. Grey's this morning. The moment he faced Him, he tells me all his doubt vanished. He cried out, 'My Lord and my God!' We have been visiting together this afternoon and evening."

"It is so wonderful," Virginia murmured. "Tell us, Mr. Stanton, something about Him. How does He look?"

"Martha described him," Stanton smiled. "He is like an average man, only different. Oh, the world, the common people, His church will receive Him. I have no question about that. They cannot help it. He is so human and brotherly. Why, do you know, He actually told two or three remarkably delightful stories while we were talking together?"

Both Virginia and Rachel looked shocked.

"Mr. Stanton!" they both exclaimed.

"And why not? Is humor ungodlike? Have not the best men we know lightened life's griefs and softened its sorrows and eased its burdens by humor? I always feel afraid of a person who does not have any."

"But it does not seem quite right—"

"Then we must change our definitions of God and divinity," Stanton said almost shortly. After a moment he added gently, "There is an indescribable charm about Him that is simply overpowering. I could not help being proud every minute that I was a Christian. And it also seemed to me every minute that I was in the presence of a person who could do most wonderful things, miracles —such as He used to do. Heal the sick, raise the dead, or walk on water."

"Do you think He will?" Rachel asked the question not without a tone of indifference, as if she were not much concerned in it.

"I do not believe He will do any wonders to satisfy any curiosity."

Rachel rose and excused herself to put her children to bed. As she went out of the room Virginia was saying: "Mr. Stanton, we are all so glad to have this great event at the time you are beginning your work here."

"It is the most astounding event of my whole life, Miss Page. What can we expect for the church from His presence?"

Virginia did not reply and Mr. Stanton rose to go.

"You will excuse me, Miss Page, I have much to do to prepare for tomorrow." He paused, then added, "I would like to have you know, Miss Page, how much I appreciate coming to First Church. Of course I know its wonderful history and the great part you and Mrs. Page and your brother and others have had in it. It will be a rare privilege to work in such an atmosphere."

Virginia was looking at the assistant pastor of the First Church with a grave, steady look as she said with direct frankness so natural to her: "We are all delighted to have you in the church to help Mr. Maxwell—and—all of us. I—we wish you every strength and blessing in it, Mr. Stanton."

"Thank you," Stanton said. He shook hands and went out. Virginia had gone to the door. When it closed, she went back into the library and stood there looking out of the window. The window commanded a view of the walk past the church. Stanton went by on this walk. What made Virginia draw back a little as his tall figure passed? Did he—turn for one moment to look at the house? Before he went on? Virginia continued to stand in the shadow after he had disappeared and was still there when Rachel came down and said, "Oh, Mr. Stanton has gone. He did not stay very long. Did you drive him away?"

"No. He had a good deal to prepare for tomorrow."

"Ah, what a day it will be, Virginia! Do you not long for it?"

"Yes, and fear it also."

"Let us not fear, but anticipate. I will sing—yes, I will sing—'Where He leads me I will follow.' "

Rachel went over to the piano and in the shadow there sat down and sang while Virginia sat in the library, her head bowed—new impulses stirring in her, new desires awakening, but in her soul knowing that deepest and best of whatever might come, the greatest was this well-nigh unthinkable coming into the world again of Jesus.

"Jesus is here!" she murmured as Rachel sang. And the refrain beat back and forth in her heart like a sweet deep-toned bell.

The people of Raymond awoke to that remarkble Sunday in its history with one thought. Long before eight o'clock the street in front of the First Church was thronged with people of all sorts. Automobiles were strung all along both sides and around the block. By the time the doors were opened, the crowd, which was more like a mob than anything else, poured in.

Mr. Maxwell's people had during the last five years remodeled the building, increasing its seating capacity to two thousand five hundred. The Sunday school departments were in special rooms below. Owing to the unusual circumstances of the service, Maxwell had directed his Sunday school officers to plan their work so that as many of the children as possible could get into the morning service.

Jasper Carter had come in time to secure a seat in the gallery. He sat there watching the great crowd pour in, a cynical smile on his hard face and the words on his lips in undertone—"What fools these mortals be!" He had not been to church for years. His paper had contained an editorial two weeks before advocating the closing of the churches as useless appendages to modern progress, meaning by "progress," material, physical, money-making human energy.

By half past nine the crowd outside was so dense and unruly that a detachment of police was on hand to preserve order. At ten o'clock the chairman of the Board of Trustees, Dr. West, rose and faced the people who were getting restless and announced that the service would shortly begin, as all the people were in the church, and that an outdoor meeting would be held at the close of the indoor service. This word was passed to the impatient crowd outdoors and did much to subdue the multitude that continued to wait and increase in numbers until the whole street was packed with an excited wall of people.

The door at the side of the pulpit platform opened and the organist, the choir, and Rachel went up into the choir loft. Then three persons came out, Mr. Maxwell, Mr. Stanton, and a third. People in the back seats of the galleries stood up. Every eye was on that third figure. And in a stillness like death or as if the audience stood at the threshold of a new chapter of human history, that unparalleled service in the First Church of Raymond began.

SOMETHING TO THINK ABOUT

1. Obviously, when Jesus was on earth two thousand years ago, He was *really* here, flesh and blood, and if cameras had been invented then, He could have had His picture taken. Why do you think Sheldon has his Jesus unable to be photographed?

2. Some of the Christians in Raymond are fearful for Jesus, knowing the world's harshness, while others re-assure them that Jesus will be able to handle everything, just as He did two thousand years ago. Do you know

Christians who seem to feel they must "protect" Christ's name from the world? If God did need this sort of defense from us, what would that say about His power?

3. Are you as uncomfortable as Rachel and Virginia were with the idea that Jesus would have a sense of humor? Why or why not?

CHAPTER IV

I t was Monday morning and Jasper Carter was in his office at the *Gazette* building talking with Barnes, his oldest reporter.

"Oh, of course I grant it was a most remarkable occasion and all that, and it will cause a sensation and make a good story, but your account of it won't do, Barnes. It simply won't do. Why, in this," Carter brought his fist down on a pile of notes on his desk, "you positively state that this person is Jesus, in person, the same Jesus who was here centuries ago."

"And He is," said Barnes.

Carter burst out angrily: "Oh look here, Barnes. That simply won't do, you know. We can't afford to be responsible for such a statement. Besides, what is the use, when we can put out just as good a story without saying that this person really is Jesus."

"But I believe He really is."

Carter sat back in his chair and eyed Barnes curiously.

"You really believe He is, do you?"

"Yes, Mr. Carter, I do. I believe it with all my mind. I do not believe any living man could have said the things He said yesterday in the First Church in the way He did."

"Do you consider the absurdity of your position, Barnes? Is it possible for such a stupendous thing as that to happen, to be a fact in this age of the world?" Carter fairly shouted.

"Why not? What has the age got to do with it?"

"Oh, it is—well, it is just sheer nonsense. Why argue? Only, I say, this story of yours is not like you, Barnes. And while it's mighty good stuff, mighty—good—stuff, it does not go in. I don't believe it, and I won't stand for it."

"You stand for a lot of things you don't believe in every day, and they go into the *Gazette* every day."

"Maybe they do," Carter retorted, red in the face, "but this does not go in. So that is settled. Strike out all this about 'firm convictions that this remarkable person is Jesus,' etc., and we can use the rest."

"You can strike them out, Mr. Carter, but I shall not because I believe every word I have written there."

"Oh well, what is the difference? When is that photograph going to be ready?"

Barnes looked at the editor of the Raymond *Gazette* with the same look that was on his face when he came into the office from Mr. Grey's on that memorable Saturday. "It is never going to be ready!"

"What! Do you mean to say we can't get a picture of this—this—person?"

"It is my honest conviction that you never will get a picture of Him for your paper."

"You have a lot of 'honest convictions' lately, Mr. Barnes." Carter spoke with a sneer. "Where did you get them?"

Barnes was on the point of saying he had never gotten them in the *Gazette* office, but after a moment, speaking with an unusual hesitation and with a heightening color, he said, "Mr. Carter, I am ready to say to you that I have come to have a firm belief in this—in Jesus Christ, and I am going to try to be a Christian."

An awkward moment followed. Then Carter said, as he broke into a short laugh, "A Christian, eh? Well, that ought to make a good 'story,' eh, Barnes?"

"It is a good story. The best I have ever heard."

"You don't really mean it?"

"Yes, I do, Mr. Carter. The greatest thing in all the world has come to me. I never knew what life meant before."

Carter frowned at him. Barnes had been a cool, hard-headed, unscrupulous news-getter, Carter's right hand for "story" writing, a man of varied mental equipment, invaluable in certain situations, not troubled with too much conscience or sensitiveness, a professional journalist of the sort that regards no one's privacy and is willing to ruin a character or pull down a reputation if necessary to get a good "story." Withal, an indefatigable worker, loyal to the *Gazette* and its policies.

Now, as Carter looked curiously at him, what did the editor see? A new man? What! In two short days? Yet that is what he did see. The miracle of transformation had come to Barnes as he sat there in the First Church looking at that tremendous personality there on the platform, listening to his words smitten down, and then lifted up again by the prayer that closed the service. He could see it now—the great throng swelling the galleries, sitting on the platform, on the floor, wherever there was a spot allowed by the fire regulations. And after the meeting, out on the church steps—when He came out there and the same unearthly hush fell over the street at the sight and sound of the man. And Barnes would never forget how, once while this was happening, He had turned His head and looked over at Barnes, the clear, calm, compelling look that had drawn him like a cable of steel into that personal discipleship that he now knew nothing could ever break. And his last view of Jesus had been that closing glimpse of Him as He walked through the crowd, His arms around the shoulders of two young men who were weeping, while the people in perfect stillness opened a way for them. And Barnes knew as he sat there in the office of the Raymond *Gazette* facing its editor, the rumble of the city coming in through the windows, he knew that nothing in all the world was so mighty as this change in purpose and passion that had come to him, and that henceforth all things were to be governed and measured by this new definition of Christian discipleship. He knew he was "born again" in that greatest of all miracles anyone has ever experienced, and that he was no more like the Barnes of last week than the robber on the cross is now like that bloody brutal figure that hung on the cross by the side of the Son of God.

But Jasper Carter was simply disturbed by what he saw in Barnes, and he anticipated something that might come up in the future. He turned in his chair and began to pick up some papers.

"When that cub, Logan, comes in, send him here," was all he remarked to Barnes.

"He has not come back since you sent him up to Mr. Maxwell's Saturday."

"Send him in if he *does* come back," Carter said shortly, and Barnes went out.

The routine of the city editor went on, interrupted this morning in the case of Mr. Carter by the thought of what had happened to Barnes. More than once he put down the papers he was reading and stared across the litter on his desk at the vision of the old Barnes transformed by the new look. Then he would shake his head and resume his work.

At the end of an hour he was called up by Barnes from the reporters' room.

"Logan is here and do you want to see him now?"

"Send him right up."

A minute later Logan came in.

The "cub" reporter looked sullen and disheveled. He was not shaved and his general appearance told several stories of failure.

"Well!" snapped out Carter in his worst humor. "What have you got?"

"Nothing."

"Then that's what you'll get. Where have you been?"

"I went to the minister's but he wouldn't let me in. I stayed up all night around the house but—He—the man—never came out. I got a seat on the platform yesterday with the folks that couldn't get any chairs, and I snapped Him twice, and I tried Him again outdoors."

"Well?"

"Someone's monkeying with my camera." The boy spoke with sullen anger.

"You mean—"

"I don't get anything. I've change my plates—"

"And you called yourself a professional photographer when you came in here."

"I am. But—"

"But what?"

"Nothing."

"That is what you are, 'but nothing.' Go back to Mr. Barnes. If he has any use for you, stay; if not, go."

The boy turned to go out. Carter called after him. "Leave your camera here. Everything."

Logan dropped his apparatus on the editor's desk and went out.

Carter eyed it with a look of incredulity.

"It is the twentieth century, and nothing is so sure as progress, money, and science. I wonder what this prince of fakers has to beat that combination? It would be worth knowing. . ."

He sat at his desk and brooded for several minutes. But his thoughts were suddenly startled by a call over the tube from Barnes. His voice was strange and full of intense feeling.

"Mr. Carter, the person—the—one—I know as Jesus is here and wants to see you."

A moment of astonishment on Carter's part. Then—

"Send Him up here."

"Very well." A pause. Then a note in Barnes's voice that Carter had never heard. "You will not—"

"I know how to be a gentleman when necessary," Carter called back, and then he faced his office door, every nerve tingling in spite of his usual proud and sneering indifference.

An hour later, Barnes, down in the reporters' room, had a sharp call from Carter.

"Come up here!"

He went up at once, and the first thing he noted when he went in was Carter's back as he bent over his desk, apparently busy over something there. As Barnes entered, he wheeled around.

"Sit down. Close the door first."

It was after he came back to the editor's desk that Barnes noted the unmistakable signs of deep agitation on Carter's face.

"Well?" Barnes did not say anything more out loud, but every fiber of him questioned the editor.

Carter spoke with evident effort. "The person—is, well, interesting, and—"

"He is more than interesting, Mr. Carter. He is really Jesus."

Carter pulled himself together. "He is just an unusually intelligent, well-bred, well-informed man. What you say, Barnes, is simply absurd. Do you know what He came to see me for?"

"No."

"He left this with me." Carter held up an ordinary typewritten manuscript. "He asked me to read it."

"Will you?"

Carter dropped the paper on his desk. "I have the usual amount of curiosity. I shall read it."

"But what—what did you talk about?"

"Well—He—spoke of seeing me in the gallery yesterday and—then—He well—" Carter laughed a little unnaturally. "He talked to me about my spiritual life. Think of that, Barnes. Who in Raymond has ever talked to me about my spiritual life? The parsons never mention it to me."

"You don't give them an opportunity."

"I didn't give—Him—an opportunity. First thing I knew we were deep in it. I will say for Him that He first asked if I had the time."

"Mr. Carter," Barnes said eagerly, "if He—really is Jesus—isn't that—I mean His talking to you about your real self, isn't that exactly what might be expected? Do you know any other person in the world who would do it?"

"No, I don't. And I don't know anyone else I would take it from. But what's the use, Barnes? He is simply an extraordinary, I will grant that, an extraordinary person with certain hypnotic gifts perhaps. But when He went out, I watched the people He passed by in the office. They didn't even turn to look at Him. Out on the sidewalk it was the same. He went His way like any average man, unnoticed."

"Perhaps it is only to those who acknowledge Him as Lord that He reveals Himself at all times. Do you remember the light?"

"Oh, that light! It is another chimera! It was just ordinary light from some astronomical phenomenon. What is the use of harking back to that!"

Barnes was silent, but he looked at Carter with a wistful gaze that belonged to the new vision of his life.

"Do you realize how long you were together, Mr. Carter?"

"No."

"It was a full hour."

"You don't say! Honestly I was really interested. He was an unusual talker. And—" As if to conceal feelings he did not want Barnes to know, Carter turned to his desk and

71

picked up Logan's camera. "I didn't get so under the spell that I missed a chance to get that picture we've wanted."

"Did you ask His consent?"

"Of course I did not."

"And you said you could be a gentleman if you had to—" Barnes began hotly.

"Keep cool now. We are in the newspaper business. Are we, or aren't we? It is our business to get the news and interest the public. This camera is the noiseless sort with the new Kydon shutter. I had it resting on this pile of books and it looked just like them. I got two good shots, and no one could tell when the thing went off. Take the plates down and develop them. We can get them ready for the four o'clock edition."

Barnes took the camera without offering a word. He hesitated as if he wanted to ask some questions but finally went away, leaving Carter seated at his desk. As he turned to look back into the office, he saw Carter pick up the manuscript and bend over his desk in his usual reading attitude.

Twenty minutes later, Carter was aware that Barnes had come in and was talking to him. How often he had spoken his name he did not know. But finally he turned around.

"These plates," Barnes was saying, "look at them—"

He held them up in front of Carter. The editor looked. There was not a line, not a shadow visible on the glass.

Henry Maxwell was pacing his study that same Monday morning while these events were occurring at the office of the Raymond *Gazette*. Grey was with him. Both men were going over the scenes of the day before.

"It was a most astonishing day all through. Grey, did you ever dream that we would see such a sight as we saw yesterday?"

"No. It seems to me now as I think back over it that it must be a dream."

As he spoke, there was a sound of voices, a man's and a woman's. A moment later Martha knocked at Mr. Maxwell's study. When he opened the door, she said: "Jesus is going downtown. He asked me to tell you He would be back for dinner."

The two men looked at her earnestly and Mr. Maxwell said, "Martha, does it not seem like a dream to you that Jesus is actually our guest and eating and sleeping in our house?"

"No, Mr. Maxwell, it does not seem like any dream to me. It is so real. And so natural. He is the most human person I ever knew. I do not feel afraid of Him as I have of some great men who have eaten and slept here."

Martha went back into the kitchen and Maxwell turned to Grey.

"Could anything be more bewildering than what Martha said just now about Jesus going downtown and coming back to dinner? Can you grasp that as a fact?"

"No. And yet, Maxwell, it is just such common things as that that were happening all the time when He was on earth before. Was it not just such things that made Him one of us? We are so overawed by our constant thought of the supernatural in Jesus that we are actually afraid of enjoying His human commonness."

" 'An average man, only different,' as Martha says. But as I sat there on the platform yesterday, I could not help asking continually, 'In what way different?' "

"He has not performed any miracles."

"Did you hear a rumor that no one has been able to get a picture of Him?"

"No. How absurd. In a scientific world of cameras and light."

"Well, I heard of it yesterday but paid little attention, there were so many other tremendous things happening. You know, Norman asked me to take notes on what He said. I was not able to put down more than the headings. Will you verify if I go over the main points?"

"Yes. I took some notes myself."

"Then we can compare. The striking thing about the whole message to me was its note of power concerning the church. 'The Gates of Death shall not prevail against it.' That seemed to ring all through the entire service like a bugle."

"Not a word, Maxwell, not a word of censure, fault finding, calling attention to the pitiful weaknesses of us preachers and our poor little discipleship. Just comfort, courage, inspiration, at the thought of the power of the church."

"Yes. But I have here a list of necessary things for the churches to do to add to the tremendous power they already possess. I don't have them in the order He mentioned them, but my notes give me these:

"First, a real union on the part of all the denominations for service. Not doctrinal or credal, but just helping to make a better world on His own working platform of love to God and others.

"Second, a definite program of the Kingdom in this age of the world. Did not your heart leap up, Grey, when He said it was the business of the churches to unite in order to have power enough together to take out of our civilization the curses of drink, lust, race prejudice, poverty, and war? What a quiet or tremendous climax that was when He pictured the new age, which He said was possible when these vices we have always regarded as a part of civilization are taken away. The hopeful thing about it all was His calm assurance that they were not necessary."

"Yes. It has only just dawned on some churches and preachers that the great vices of humanity are less powerful than the gospel."

"Then I have—Third, the possibility of a printed message every day to represent the church and its great work. We have no daily paper to speak for us. What would Christianity have been all these centuries without a Bible? Yet here we are today in a world of the daily printed page without anything to speak daily the message of Christianity, as it really is. We need such an organ, not only for proclaiming God's righteousness but for information concerning the greatness of the gospel in its worldwide conquest."

"I note in connection with that, His statement that the editors and owners of daily papers owe it to civilization that they use their papers to advance all human causes. If every great daily in all the great cities of the United States would help the church and the home in their battle with the world's gross vices there would not be a brewery or a saloon or a house of vice left in these cities at the end of ten years."

"What a splendid sweep of power went over the audience at that! I tell you, Grey, it seemed to me at that point I felt as I never did before the everlasting might of Jesus in action. All things seemed possible."

"But did you notice, sitting directly in front of Jesus, up in the gallery, was Carter of the *Gazette*? Does it seem possible to you that a man of Carter's ambitions will ever use his newspaper for Christian purposes? Remember how he has fought Norman and the churches all these years."

"He will never change the policy of the *Gazette* until he himself is changed. I dread the appearance of the *Gazette* tonight. No doubt Barnes will have a 'story' in it that will be full of irreverence and sensationalism. Think of the caricatures Jesus will have to endure."

"He endured them while He was here before. Who understood Him then? Not even His own disciples. The cultured and the leaders in society and the high and mighty hated and jeered and finally crucified. It was the 'common people' that heard Him gladly. Can we expect it to be different now?"

"Yes. Because there are all the accumulations of centuries of martyrdom and discipleship between then and now. Grey, we live in an infinitely better world than was here when Jesus lived before. Did He not say so Himself? It is that note in His message of yesterday that is going to give this age wings of courage and hope. The worst thing the devil has done for the churches this last quarter of a century has been to preach the doctrine of pessimism."

Mr. Maxwell was interrupted by a telephone ring. It was a call from Rollin Page, who had just gotten back from Chicago. He had called up Mr. Maxwell to say that their little girl Eloise was very sick.

"What!" Mr. Maxwell exclaimed, shocked by the sudden news. "Oh, I am deeply sorry for you. Don't get anxious. Yes, I knew Rachel was staying with Virginia while you were away. Dr. West is always splendid with children. Yes. I'll come right over."

As he hung up the receiver, he turned a serious look at Grey. "Rollin says Eloise is very ill. She was not feeling very well when Rachel put her to bed Saturday. Yesterday morning she was worse but insisted on her mother coming to sing. And oh how Rachel did sing, yesterday, Grey. It reminded me of sixteen years ago. And this morning Rollin says the change in the child is so alarming they have called in Jackson and Oswald to consult with West. Rachel is nearly beside herself. I must go right over."

Grey said something by way of sympathy for Rollin and Rachel, and as Maxwell was going out, he walked along with him. As they turned the corner leading to Virginia's house, Grey suddenly paused and put his hand on Maxwell's arm.

"In case—do you suppose—if He knew—would He—do anything?"

"Who?" said Maxwell, who had been musing over the events of the last two days.

"Jesus. Would He not be able to cure Eloise? How do we know what power He has over disease and death?"

"Grey, I have been thinking of all that, together with any number of things that His coming suggests. How little we really know about Him yet! But if He has the power, why should He not use it? Why not? Why not?

77

Rachel—how she does love those children—yes, I see no reason why He would not help them if He can."

Maxwell hurried on to Virginia's, leaving Grey standing on the corner looking after him.

Before he rang the bell, someone opened the door; and the moment he stepped into the hall, he felt the passing chill of that breath that blows off the coast of Death. Before he had reached the foot of the stairs, Virginia was there. Her face told the story.

"A few minutes ago," her lips whispered. "The doctors think it was poison. A mystery. But oh, Mr. Maxwell, I am afraid for Rachel. Go to her."

Mr. Maxwell went upstairs. Rollin met him at the door of the room. He was remarkably calm, but Death in coming so near had left an imprint on his face and in his eyes. He laid his head on Mr. Maxwell's breast and groaned.

"Come in," he managed to say after a moment. "I don't know what will happen to Rachel."

Rachel was on her knees, her arms flung out across the bed. The three doctors were standing at the foot of it. Dr. West had tried to get Rachel out of the room. She had fought him like an animal and at last flung herself down as Mr. Maxwell now saw her.

He went up, put his hand on her head, and said gently, "Rachel!"

There was no movement for a minute. Then Rachel moved her shoulders convulsively and slowly turned her head and looked up.

Mr. Maxwell kneeled by her side. Rachel was tearless. But in the midst of the prayer that Maxwell began to offer, she suddenly turned on her knees and caught Mr. Maxwell's arm.

"Oh!" she exclaimed. "I have just thought! Mr. Maxwell! Have you forgotten? Have you forgotten? Jesus is here! Send for Him! He can bring Eloise to life! Send for Him! Jesus is here!"

She rose to her feet and dragged almost fiercely at Mr. Maxwell. The doctors looked at one another. Mr. Maxwell tried to calm Rachel. But she seemed like one distracted. She kept exclaiming, "Send for Him, Mr. Maxwell! Won't you? Send at once!"

Dr. West came over to Maxwell.

"Where is—He—"

"At my house probably by this time."

"I'll call Him," Dr. West said briefly.

He went out into the upper hall and called up Maxwell's house. Martha answered. A few sentences were exchanged.

Then Dr. West came back into the death chamber.

"He will be here soon," was all the doctor said.

Rachel fell on her knees again and this time without any violent outburst she said as she folded her hands together: "Jesus is here! He will bring my child to life again! Jesus is here! Oh, thank God, He is here!"

Then there was silence in that chamber. Mr. Maxwell's lips were moving in prayer for Rachel and Rollin while they all waited for His coming.

SOMETHING TO THINK ABOUT

1. Remember, this story is an allegory, not a description of something that might actually happen. What do you think Sheldon is saying when only those who acknowledge the lordship of Jesus are able to recognize Him when He walks among them?

2. The characters in this story are almost shocked by Jesus doing something as ordinary as going downtown. Do you exclude Christ from the everyday, trivial events of your life? Or do you recognize His presence even in the common, ordinary occurrences?

CHAPTER V

T hree days had passed, and Rachel and Rollin stood side by side at a grave. The coffin was just being lowered. As the top of it sank to a level with the grass, the lilies on it looked as though they were growing in that spot. Rachel with Rollin's arm about her leaned upon him. At the head of the grave stood Mr. Maxwell and Mr. Grey and Virginia was near, but next to Rachel stood the figure of the Man.

Rachel turned her eyes up to Him as Mr. Maxwell finished reading the service:

"Now the God of peace who brought again from the dead the great shepherd of the sheep with the blood of the eternal covenant, even our Lord Jesus, make you perfect in every good thing to do His will, working in us that which is well-pleasing in His sight, through Jesus Christ; to whom be glory for ever and ever. Amen."

The Man stood there, tears on His face—and yet—and yet—as Rachel looked—

She recalled His coming into Eloise's sick room, how she fell at His feet and besought Him to give her back her darling—and—all that followed—

What was it all?

It mingled with her whole sense of life's mysteries—this thing called death. What was it He had said—

Would she and Rollin lose all their faith in a heavenly

Father unless Eloise were brought to life? Did their faith in Him rest upon His answer to this one petition or did it rest upon something more vital and fundamental? If He were to say He would not use His power to bring the child to life, on account of reasons they could not now understand, would they curse God and die? Or would they accept even death as a part of the human life and go on to live their lives even more strongly and beautifully on account of it? One thing He could promise, that no cloud of doubt would ever obscure their vision of Eloise alive and happy in a world far above this one in joy and beauty. Of that they would always be assured.

And there were other words spoken, which blended into all the rest more or less vaguely in Rachel's heart and mind. But the main thing, the sharp distinct fact remained. Eloise, her child, was dead. Jesus had not brought her to life. Why? Why? Was He, then, not real? Was it not Jesus after all?

But no, Rachel found, even in that most heart-breaking moment of all funerals—when the coffin holding what she held dearest was sinking down into the ground—even at that moment, as she looked up at Him, that she did not doubt. Jesus was there by her side. She believed in Him. Her faith was triumphant.

The tears had come at last, to her relief. Through them she saw her friends, she saw her husband with whom she was passing through their first great sorrow—and irresistibly again and again she returned with her thought and her look to Him, yes, to Him who for some good reason had denied her heart-breaking appeal and had not performed a miracle for her sake.

When the service at the cemetery was all over and Rachel and Virginia and Rollin and Dr. West and Mr. and Mrs. Maxwell had gone together to Rollin's home, Jesus was not there. Mr. Maxwell did not know where He was, and his mind was in a tumult over His sudden disappearance. But to his amazement and the wonder of Rollin and all the rest, Rachel seemed to understand, and her whole bearing was that of calm and even joyful confidence. She was holding the boy, Frank, in her lap and saying to Mr. Maxwell:

"I do not have any doubt of His character, His person, or His wisdom. My heart is at rest for Eloise. Do not fear for me. My mind was distracted; Jesus has comforted me. Oh, I begin to see how it is possible for some things to surpass even death and its blows. Yes, I believe in Him wholly. Eloise is alive and happy. I asked Him to give her back to me alive. He is doing more than that. He is making me certain that she is alive in a better world than this."

"Mr. Maxwell," said Rollin, while tears flowed over his face, "do you hear that? And yet— What is Jesus' teaching about disease? Did He not heal when He was here before? Will He not do the same now?"

Mr. Maxwell bowed his head, troubled in thought.

"I must confess my faith in Jesus is somewhat shaken. I really thought when He came the other day that He would perform a mighty work. I cannot understand why He did not. But concerning His power over disease, do you not remember, Doctor, what He said to us yesterday and the day before?"

Dr. West spoke eagerly. "Yes! His general attitude

toward disease will be that the world is learning how to control and eradicate the causes of disease by finding out the reasons. For Him to heal a few diseased people would be a small thing compared with directing human energy and research toward the causes of human suffering and finally removing them. And that, as I understand Him, is going to be His attitude toward the whole problem of disease."

"All that would not hinder Him from healing suffering people, and He may do that," Maxwell said, still troubled as he looked at Rollin and Rachel and remembered their grief. "Dearly Beloved, what can I say to you? Surely in all this mystery of death in life even for the little children, God's love is going to be revealed to us."

"I do not question His love," Rachel answered bravely. "I did at first. But Jesus has comforted me. I do not question His wisdom or His love. Somehow I feel that His coming will mean to the world vastly more than the bringing to life again of even our dear one." And Rachel laid her face down on the boy's fair head while her tears fell, but they were tears of faith, not of despair or bitterness.

"Where do you suppose He can have gone?" Maxwell asked in a low tone of Grey.

"I do not know. He returned with me as far as my house. You know I have asked the privilege of having Him with me tonight. But when I turned to go in with Him before coming up here, He was gone."

There was silence among the friends. Even the solemn and awful stroke of death had not been able to lessen their tremendous interest in this coming into their homes and their lives of Jesus. His every act and word, His daily plans,

His future plans, His attitude toward all the varied interests of the human life around Him was fascinating to them.

Yet even while all that was true, as Mr. Maxwell said, speaking with wondering interest, Raymond was already beginning to accept His presence as if it were almost commonplace. Only as the news of His coming had gone out over the country, a general wave of curiosity and inquiry was pulsing into Raymond, but among the churches and the ministers His presence was hardly realized. Only a small number of people had as yet heard Him speak. Mr. Maxwell had arranged a conference with all the churches and pastors, which was to be held the next day in the First Church. Deep interest was being shown in this, and Mr. Maxwell was busy every moment answering calls, making inquiries about this meeting. He himself was anticipating it with keenest wonder at its probable results. But within the last two days his faith had been shaken. This person calling Himself Jesus, who had moved the people so wonderfully in the church Sunday and at the outdoor service, was walking the streets of Raymond like an average man, attracting no special attention, talking with everyone indiscriminately, playing with children, entering into the commonplaces of Raymond like any common man; and when a supreme test had come to show a real power, He had failed; or at least He had refused to exhibit anything that could distinguish Him for others. Was He really Jesus? Where were the signs and wonders?

Mr. Maxwell, searching his own feeling, going over every word and act of the Man, could not call up one single thing that did not somehow belong naturally to Jesus.

Neither could he detect one single weakness or fault in Him. And while he wavered in his judgment of some things he had observed, he was staggered as he viewed the calm courage and unshaken faith of Rachel and Rollin.

All this only made him the more eager to see and know more of the Person who had in less than a week become the one absorbing object of his heart and mind.

What would He do next? What plans had He for the church? How would He answer all the hard questions the people were beginning to ask? When would He begin to heal? What part would He take as a citizen in the regular duties of the municipality? What would He say about business and amusements and education?

These and many other queries tumultuously surged through Mr. Maxwell's mind as he looked into the future.

He was still going over all this on his way home from Rollin and Rachel's and had only just gone into his study when he was called up by Barnes from the *Gazette* office.

"Mr. Carter wants to know if you can come up to the office. He wants to see you on a special matter."

"I can come now as well as any time."

"Very well. Mr. Carter would like to see you."

Fifteen minutes later Mr. Maxwell was in the *Gazette* editor's office, facing him and wondering what he wanted.

During all the years of Maxwell's pastorate in Raymond extending over twenty years, Edward Norman, a member of Maxwell's church, and Jasper Carter, a non-church man, had been rival newspapermen. The *News* was a morning paper, independent in politics, ready to give its aid to all good reforms, and a steady distinctive force for law and order.

The *Gazette* was managed by Carter on the principle that seems to govern many large city dailies where sensationalism and exaggeration of crime, scandal, and sin are the leading features. Carter had always opposed the churches and had boasted more than once that he could drive any man out of his pulpit if he got too radical with the preaching of reform. He had fought for the saloon when it was in danger of being voted out, and when it was finally outlawed, he still advocated high license and insisted on personal liberty. He was for the segregation of vice and a police force armed with clubs and guns. He was specially bitter and hostile to all preachers and often spoke of them in his editorials as "non-producers." He gloried in "progress" and defined it in terms of money-making and success. In short, he had made out of his paper a money-getting investment and was proud of his influence in Raymond.

It is not therefore strange that Mr. Maxwell wondered why Carter should wish to see him. On his way to the office, he connected the editor's request with the coming of Jesus. And Carter's first words spoken politely enough showed him that his surmise was correct.

"I wanted to see you, Mr. Maxwell, about this—this person who calls Himself Jesus. I understand He is staying with you. Are you willing to tell me what you think of Him?"

It was characteristic of Carter's effrontery that he had not the slightest hesitation about using anyone for his own advantage if he thought he could get anything out of him for his paper. It made no difference to him that he had sneered at men like Maxwell all his life and cast contempt on the church and all it stood for.

Mr. Maxwell understood the character of the man completely.

"Mr. Carter, I may say frankly I don't care to talk about Him for any publication. I have already refused to be interviewed on the subject by the representatives of other papers."

"But I notice the *News* seems to have inside information. I suppose you give to your own flock what you do not give to strangers on the outside."

"I have not talked to any newspapermen about Him. Whatever has appeared in the *News* does not contain any quotations or opinions of mine."

"I suppose you have noticed the different views expressed by different people in town about this person's outward appearance? Does that strike you as peculiar?"

"Mr. Carter, if you requested me to come here to talk about—this—person, I wish to say again, frankly, I do not care to talk to you about Him."

"To me?"

"To you or any other newspaperman."

"Why not?" Carter was beginning to get angry.

"I don't think it necessary to give reasons." Mr. Maxwell rose to go.

But Carter smiled blandly and said: "Don't go, Mr. Maxwell. I have an interesting statement to make that I am sure will deeply concern you. Have you noticed that up to the present time not a single picture of—of—this person calling Himself Jesus has appeared in any paper? Do you realize that such a thing is an astonishing fact?"

Mr. Maxwell could not help saying it was.

"I don't mind telling you, Mr. Maxwell, that, as no doubt you would expect, the *Gazette* has tried to get a picture, but so far has failed."

Mr. Maxwell was saying silently, *For which failure I am deeply thankful.*

"And I don't mind saying, in fact, that is one reason I wanted to see you—that I myself tried to get a picture of—Him, but my plates are clear—no negative."

Mr. Maxwell made no comment. Carter looked at him sharply.

"Is not that a curious thing? How do you account for it?"

"I don't account for it."

Carter was silent a moment, as if measuring how far he could go. Then he said with a great show of frankness, "Mr. Maxwell, could you do me a favor? I understand, of course, we have not always been on your side and all that, but we've always fought in the open, and—well—while I've no use for the preachers generally, I've always had respect for your consistency. Now you're near to this person; what is the reason you couldn't get the secret of this rather remarkable feat of beating a camera, and let us have it? Or why shouldn't you find out why His picture can't be taken or, better yet, get one for us? I promise you, Mr. Maxwell, I will treat the matter sensibly—or my head reporter will, Mr. Barnes, and by the way he claims to be a convert, really believes it is Jesus and all that—he will write up a 'story' in your own style, if you will help out, you know. Besides it's your teaching, you know, to forgive your enemies! What better chance can you have than right now? I don't mind saying very frankly that the reason I want this picture is to beat the other papers. Correspondents are headed this way from all over the country. Why should we let them get ahead of our own local press?"

The first feeling that came over Maxwell while Carter was speaking was one of intense anger. But as Carter paused, he controlled himself enough to say calmly: "You will have to excuse me, Mr. Carter, for refusing to do what you ask. I may as well say I don't believe in your journalistic methods and I can't be a party to them."

Carter bounded up out of his chair in one of his sudden bursts of rage.

"And you call yourself a Christian? You're one of these whining, sanctimonious 'holier than thou' preachers who go around, measuring up all other persons with their little standards of conduct, nonentities themselves in the general world of progress and—"

Mr. Maxwell had risen and he simply said, "Good day, Mr. Carter," and walked out of the office. As he opened the door, he ran into Barnes, who from the look on his face had evidently caught a part of Carter's remarks, as the editor had raised his voice. Barnes gave Maxwell a glance of respect and then went on into the office.

Carter was standing by his desk, white-lipped and snarling, but he turned about before Barnes could speak and began pawing over things on his desk.

"I have brought up that manuscript you wanted me to read," Barnes said. "You told me to bring it back as soon as I was through with it."

"Well?" Carter's "Well?" could mean almost anything according to his mood. Barnes ignored it and went on.

"It's the most remarkable manuscript I ever read, Mr. Carter. What are you going to do with it?"

"I don't know yet. Leave it here."

Barnes put it down on the editor's desk, and then, judging from Carter's looks that he did not want to talk, he started to go out. Just as he got to the door, Carter called him back.

"Why shouldn't I publish the thing in the *Gazette*?"

"You could, of course, but—"

"But what?"

"It contradicts everything the paper stands for."

"What of that?"

"I don't believe you would dare print it."

"I dare do anything I like for the paper." Carter spoke irritably. Then, calming down, he said: "See here, Barnes. This—this—person you believe is Jesus—annoys me. I've got out of sorts over Him. I might as well confess to you that this mystery of the cameras haunts me. The correspondents of a dozen big papers are coming in here tomorrow. Some of them will reach here tonight. Now, it's incredible that modern journalism will fall down over this picture business. I want you to go to this meeting Maxwell has arranged for Him tomorrow, and by hook or crook secure a picture. I don't care how you get it, but get it. I tried to wheedle Maxwell into helping us out, but he didn't rise to flattery and—"

"Was that flattery I heard as I came in?"

"Well, no—I lost myself a little. You know my failing, but this little matter of the negatives has got on my nerves and—well—you have got to get busy and secure that picture at any costs. I count on you, Barnes. Find out the trick. For, of course, it's a trick all right."

"I do not believe it is a trick, Mr. Carter. . . ." Barnes spoke slowly.

"Not a trick! What—"

"I must say also that I cannot do what you ask. I believe with all my soul that this is Jesus actually come to earth again. I do not believe I have any right to exploit His person in the paper. If for His own good reasons He chooses to defend Himself from the impertinence of the press I will not—"

"Impertinence!" Carter's voice cut across Barnes's sentence with rough insistence. "What have you been doing all your life but getting the photographs of famous people whether they liked it or not? It is our business. It is all in the day's work."

"It is not in my day's work anymore, Mr. Carter."

"What's the matter with you?"

"I told you, Mr. Carter, I have become a Christian. I am His disciple."

Carter suppressed an oath. Then after a pause—

"Do you mean to say, Barnes, that you actually believe this person is Jesus Christ, the same person who was here nineteen hundred years ago?"

"I believe it with all my soul."

"Your soul?"

"Yes."

"You never mentioned your soul before. I never heard of it all these years. Barnes, do you really believe such a stupendous thing could happen?"

"It has happened."

"Barnes, you are a fool!"

92

Barnes made no reply.

"You're a fool!"

"I'm willing to be one."

"But I don't know that I'm willing to have one on the *Gazette*. One of us will have to go off the payroll."

"I'm ready to go anytime."

"Oh look here, Barnes. You can't really believe such an absurdity. It would be a miracle."

"It is a miracle."

"Miracle? There isn't any such thing."

"Why not?"

"In this age?"

"Why not? What has the age got to do with it?"

"To do with it!" Carter exploded. "You're a fool."

"You have said it three times, but it does not make me one."

Carter struck his desk with his fist. "This person you believe is Jesus is a fake. I will make it my business to expose Him."

"And yet you cannot with all your boasted progress and science get His picture."

"That is a trick."

"It is a miracle."

Carter got up quickly from his desk. "Barnes, if He is really Jesus as you say, why did He not prove it the other day by bringing to life Mrs. Page's little girl? Didn't you hear that they begged Him to do that and He refused?"

"I don't know why. But I don't rest my faith in Him on any mighty works He may do."

"You don't! What do you rest it on?"

"On Himself. I believe in Him."

Carter was walking up and down. He stopped, looked at Barnes sharply, then suddenly put his hand on his shoulder and said frankly: "Barnes, old man, you've been on the *Gazette* a long time. How many years is it?"

"Fifteen."

"And you've come to be invaluable to me. You've stayed by the job and you've been faithful to the *Gazette* and its policy. I hate to see you going off on this tangent. You're deluded."

"I have been all these years, Mr. Carter. But not now. For the first time in my life I see clearly."

Carter moved over to his desk and sat down. Then he said coldly, "You refuse to do what I ask, then?"

"Yes. I can't do it."

A pause. Then—

"One of us will have to go, Barnes. We are not running a Sunday school here."

"I expect I had better go, anyway, Mr. Carter. There are too many things in the paper that I can't agree with anymore and they will be making trouble between us right along."

"You can stay through your month," Carter said shortly. "At the end of that time I can prove to you that you are a fool and you will want to stay with the *Gazette*."

Barnes looked at the editor earnestly. The new Barnes. What a wonder that Carter did not see right there in front of him a miracle greater than a dead person raised to life! But his eyes were blind that he should not see.

Barnes went out gently, and Carter sat moodily staring at the things on his desk, but not seeing them.

Suddenly he seized the manuscript Barnes had

brought back, opened it, and for the fourth time began to read it. It was the most astonishing manuscript he had ever read.

In the first place the beauty of the manuscript was beyond anything Jasper Carter had ever known. In all his experience as an editor, as a writer of brilliant editorials and pungent paragraphs, he had never read anything equal to it. Neither could he recall any standard author of any race who had ever written anything to equal it.

Added to beauty of expression was also an astounding knowledge of history and humanity. It was so marked, it was overwhelming. Nothing like it in all ancient or modern literature had ever come under his observation.

At the close of the manuscript were some verses, so exquisite, so marvelously constructed that he held his breath as he read them over. Something in them stirred even his dull imagination, as if into that prosaic newspaper office had come the fragrant beat of an angel's wing. The indescribable harmony and pathos and charm of the lines defied analysis and criticism. Something in them gripped his heart. He had always denied the supernatural and spiritual. But what was this within him that in spite of himself acknowledged a subtle something different from mere human intellect and knowledge?

He rose greatly excited and seizing the paper lifted it up with his powerful hands as if to tear it in pieces. He knew he dared not, yes, dared not print this marvelous manuscript in his paper. The entire thing was a direct and overwhelming blow at his entire newspaper and editorial policy. It was so perfect and clear a scathing rebuke of all the methods he had pursued all his life that every reader of the *Gazette* reading it would see in every line the selfish, hypocritical, self-centered, unscrupulous editor of the paper. It would make him the butt of scoffing from every newspaper in the country, even from those journals that were like his own. And he knew it. For the manuscript held him, himself, up to himself as he was. With all its unrivaled beauty of style and marvelous splendor of expression, he knew as he read that he dared not for his own peace of mind in the future publish the manuscript in his own paper. Yet there it lay, containing words that would make any paper that could print it famous all over the world.

He walked up and down restlessly. This—this—person had not asked him to publish the manuscript in the *Gazette*. He had simply asked him to read it, if he had time. That was all. Why? Why? To reveal him to himself? To reveal to his own narrow self-centered person his own little soul bound in the fetters of custom and gross money-grabbing and pitiful ambition?

He snarled as he walked, like some wild animal that is caged and starved.

"I will expose this fake! No man who lives shall get the better of me with tricks like these. If Barnes is willing to be a fool, I'm not. I'll go to this meeting tomorrow and—"

He turned, went back to his desk, took up the manuscript, looked at it as if fascinated, then suddenly picked it up, thrust it into a pigeon hole of his desk, and with a grim smile resumed his regular work.

Meanwhile Mr. Maxwell, on leaving the *Gazette* office, had gone directly to the hotel where Stanton was staying until arrangements could be made by Dr. West to give him rooms in his home. Maxwell found Stanton just opening his mail.

"I have, as you have, a great many letters making inquiry about—Him. I hardly know how to answer all the questions. And yet—"

"And yet?" asked Maxwell.

"I have no doubt. Have not had at any time. I was out on the street a little while ago. What do you think I saw as I went by the municipal playgrounds?"

Maxwell was silent.

"He was out there playing with the children."

"Why not?" Maxwell murmured after a silence.

"Why not? Just what I said." Stanton asked Maxwell to excuse him and then went on opening letters.

He read a letter, glanced at Maxwell with a deep look of interest, and handed the letter over.

"Chancellor Clark wants you to invite Jesus to speak at the university regular assembly tomorrow morning! Will He go?"

"I have no doubt of it," Stanton replied. "You see the chancellor asks me to come with Him and be on the platform. I have not been to the university since I graduated. I have never met Clark."

"You know him, though?"

"Only what I have heard."

Maxwell was silent.

"I am surprised he has asked Jesus to speak to the students."

"Why?"

"They have no regular chapel service at the university

any longer and Clark is not a religious man. What does he expect Jesus will talk about to the students?"

"I don't know." Stanton sat there very thoughtful. "Of course he must know Jesus has only one theme—"

"I see by the letter," Maxwell spoke with quickening interest, "that the chancellor asks you both to take luncheon with him just before chapel service."

"Yes."

"The last time I had luncheon with the chancellor he had three kinds of liquor on the table, and—"

Stanton looked thoughtfully at Maxwell.

"The atmosphere at the university does not seem the same as when I was there."

"No. Since the state put the Bible out of the schools, many things are different. Many of the professors at the university are non-Christian men. I think in my time, forty years ago, every teacher was at least a professed Christian."

There was another thoughtful silence as Stanton and Maxwell looked at each other.

"You remember you are due at the afternoon conference at the church at three-thirty?"

"Yes. We shall be back from the university in ample time. Dr. West has asked me to call at his house at two o'clock to look over his rooms. I shall of course be glad to get away from this hotel and be settled in more homelike quarters."

"Stanton, you ought to have a home of your own."

"I know it." Over Stanton's strong noble face a natural glow of color passed. "Perhaps I shall have some time. Would it seem—well—strange to you if I were to say what

98

you said just now is what Jesus said to me yesterday, as we were going over to look at the new city hospital? He said it just as naturally as you did just now."

"Why not?"

"That's what I said at the time. Why not?"

"Stanton, we're living in the midst of astonishing events, and no one can foresee the end. I anticipate some remarkable scenes at the university tomorrow. I wish I could go with you, but I shall be busy every minute getting ready for the conference."

"Will the ministers all come?"

"Yes, and from all I can judge now, I don't believe the church will begin to hold the people. Do you realize, Stanton, that the attention of the whole country is being directed to Raymond? The newspaper representatives of more than forty papers will be here tonight. You will no doubt have many of them out at the university tomorrow. But when you are through over there, let Jesus come to my house and rest before the conference while you keep your appointment with Dr. West."

"Come to your house and *rest*?"

"Yes. Have you not noticed He gets weary just as you and I do? Did you not see how tired He was after that tremendous outdoor service Sunday afternoon?"

"Yes. But why should He—"

"Grow tired? Have you forgotten Him at Jacob's well? Is He not the same here?"

" 'The same yesterday, today, and forever,' " murmured Stanton. "I'll do as you say and insist on His going to your house to rest. How strange! To insist on Jesus doing something! Maxwell, are we dreaming? Shall we awake soon to

99

the old common-places we used to know?"

"I think not. It is all too amazingly real. But I would give anything to go with you tomorrow. It will be a great meeting, that with the students and—the chancellor."

"I'm sure of it," Stanton said. His excitement was rising.

He vaguely imagined what might happen, but not even his glowing imagination could picture the reality as it occurred the next day out there at the university assembly, after that luncheon with the chancellor and several of the faculty members.

Those unparalleled scenes at the university had come and gone; he had returned to the city with Jesus and had seen Him walking calmly toward Mr. Maxwell's house, while he himself, every nerve in him tingling with most thrilling feeling, walked over to Dr. West's to keep his appointment about the rooms where he anticipated making his future home with the doctor who was Virginia's uncle, an old bachelor who had welcomed the possibility of having this strong young preacher in his house with him.

But not even when he went in and was greeted heartily by the doctor did he seem to be conscious of the object of his being there. And not even when Virginia appeared in the drawing room did he seem to hear Dr. West saying, "Virginia, Miss Page, my niece, you know, has just come over to see if her old uncle is behaving himself in his bachelor quarters. Nothing like having someone like Virginia to look after you, eh, Stanton?"

Not even the doctor's impersonal use of the embarrassing pronoun "you" nor Virginia's deep blush as she turned to say something to the doctor seemed to rouse Stanton.

"Yes," he said vaguely. "Excuse me, but I have just been through a most astonishing scene at the university. I cannot think of anything else just now."

"Oh!" exclaimed Virginia eagerly. "Tell us about it. He spoke there to the students?"

"Yes," said Stanton slowly. "Yes."

He was silent. A full minute passed, one of those silences with which people were fast growing familiar.

A rush of sound swept into the house from the street. Dr. West was standing near the window and was looking out eagerly.

"Looks like the whole university."

Stanton rose, and Virginia, and side by side they looked out. A tumultuous crowd was flowing by, shouting, waving pennants, and gesticulating. It seemed to the doctor and Virginia that the student body was divided into two hostile groups.

"They are headed for the church," Stanton said after a while.

"We ought to be going, Uncle," said Virginia. "We won't be able to get in."

"Mr. Maxwell will find places for us. This conference is for the church people specially and was so announced. I want to hear from Mr. Stanton what occurred out at the university."

"It must have been—" Virginia began.

Stanton came back from the window and sat down. "It was the most remarkable scene in a university I ever witnessed and confirms all my faith in Him. May I wait a moment?" He spoke to Virginia, who was leaning forward in an attitude of intense expectancy. "And I will tell as well as I can what occurred out there at the university." Virginia and Dr. West leaned forward with intense interest to listen and Stanton went on.

SOMETHING TO THINK ABOUT

1. Why do you think Jesus failed to heal Rachel and Rollin's little girl?

2. Have you ever had an experience when you thought Jesus would work a certain way in your life, and He failed to do so? How did this experience affect your faith?

3. Sheldon has mentioned several times the strange silence that comes over people as a result of Jesus' presence. Have you ever experienced this sort of quiet moment when you felt Christ was near to you?

Chapter VI

F irst of all," Stanton began, "as soon as we reached the
chancellor's we went right out to luncheon. Six of
the professors were present. Do you know Chancellor
Clark very well?" He stopped abruptly to ask the question
of Dr. West.

"No. Not very."

"Neither do I. I went out there determined to carry
an unbiased mind. Chancellor Clark is a smart man. A
great lobbyist for the university. And all that. But I had
wondered why he wanted a person like Jesus to speak to
the students.

"I soon found out. He was present Sunday morning
at the church, and from some things said there, he judged
that Jesus would deliver an interesting address to the students and add to its reputation. The chancellor, I am told,
has always been eager to get celebrities to appear at the
university."

Dr. West nodded.

"Mr. Maxwell had prepared me for the habits of the
chancellor, so I was not surprised at seeing the liquor and
tobacco at the luncheon. But I was surprised when Jesus
appeared to take no notice of them in any way."

"Did He—"

"No. He did not touch them. But He said nothing
about them either. It is not possible to describe in detail

His talk at the table. I have never heard anything like it anywhere. We have very few great talkers nowadays. He did not monopolize the conversation, but He led it out, and every man at the table did his best.

"But nothing unusual occurred, and the strange thing I could not avoid thinking about was that no one seemed particularly impressed with the tremendous fact that Jesus was actually the guest of the university. I believe the only impression those men, including the chancellor, received, was of a clever, distinguished man of modest bearing, who was perhaps unusually well informed, but in other respects not so very far superior to any one of them.

"When the luncheon was over and we were in the auditorium facing the student body, it seemed to me that something unusual was about to occur. First of all, Jesus had requested of the chancellor that he omit all words of introduction. This was while we were seated at the table. When the time came for the address, the chancellor evidently intended to pay no attention to this request. He rose and began by a reference to 'our distinguished guest' and was apparently going on with a long speech when it seemed to me, and I think it must have been the same with the others, Jesus began addressing the students as if the chancellor were not present, and yet it did not strike me as in any way rude or discourteous. It all seemed so natural that no one seemed to be questioning Jesus' right to act just as He did.

"For the next ten minutes I think it is safe to say that every person in that great audience was simply overwhelmed by the eloquence of the Master. But do we not remember the instance of the attempt to arrest Him while He was speaking in the Temple? And do we not recall the astonishing fact that the Roman officers themselves dared not touch Him and came back to those who had sent them, giving as their excuse, 'Never man spake like this man'?

"I do not believe the world has ever given Jesus credit for overpowering eloquence as a public speaker. But I do know that during those first ten minutes there was not a person of the thirty-five hundred present who did not feel moved as he had never felt in all his life by a public speaker.

"Suddenly, He turned to the chancellor and asked him a question concerning the habits of a certain number of the students in the university. The chancellor was simply dumbfounded. I sat where I could distinctly see him, and I think I have never observed on any man's face such a look of anger and conviction combined.

"It was as still as death all over the great hall. The voice of Jesus (have we not all spoken of its marvelous power and beauty?) thrilled everyone. And I think I felt, I think all felt, a real fear such as no human being ever inspired; at least I never had such a feeling in the presence of anyone as I had today, the fear of a sinful man in the presence of perfect righteousness.

"Jesus' question was one He had a perfect right to ask. If the National Education Association is right in saying as it did two years ago that 'the great end and aim of all education is character,' then surely Jesus has a right to call the chancellor to account for his tremendous influence in the matter of his own example before his own students."

"In the matter of the liquor and the tobacco?" Virginia was saying eagerly.

"Yes. In the plainest language he called the chancellor to account for the personal example he was daily living before his own students, an example so contrary to that of a great educator of youth that no excuse could be offered and the only reparation he could make would be to repent and cleanse his physical life of all such habits.

"Then came the scene which the papers no doubt will emphasize the most. And by the way, there must have been over twenty press representatives there from over the country."

"Yes," Dr. West spoke. "Norman tells me the town will be full of them by tomorrow. This scene at the university will bring many more."

"But this is only the beginning. As I was saying, the chancellor sat there while Jesus was condemning him, white with anger and conviction. Suddenly he stood up and exclaimed in a terrible voice, 'Leave the platform, you insolent—'

"I did not hear the word that followed. But after one tremendous moment of deathly stillness, the students all over the assembly hall raised a cry of remonstrance. 'Fair play! Fair play! Let Him finish!'

"Then, to my mind, followed what seemed to me the most remarkable scene of all the day. He turned to the student body and began to speak as if the chancellor were not present and had not said a word. I believe at that moment I had some glimpse of Jesus' real power as 'Lord of all.' As for the chancellor—I do not know yet what his action meant, but after Jesus began talking to the student body again, he turned and walked off of the stage. The rest of the faculty members looked simply dazed at the whole affair, but they sat there on the platform gazing at Jesus as if awestruck.

"As He went on talking to the students, I realized that another scene was impending, this time with the students. For as Jesus went on, He began to condemn the fraternities in the university, which were destroying the social democracy of the place. He seemed to know exactly what the conditions were, and looks of amazement were everywhere among the students as He went on to give detailed accounts of their social affairs, their wine suppers, and especially a recent carouse at the close of an athletic contest which had been a disgrace to the state.

"I shall never forget how groups of the students sat there white-faced and enraged as Jesus went on. And every minute I looked for some outburst, but the silence seemed to deepen as Jesus calmly but with awful directness spoke of the coarse dissipation and selfish exclusiveness of large student groups.

"Suddenly He turned to the faculty members on the platform and to their bewilderment asked them what could be expected of students if those who were set over them as teachers and counselors were men of disbelief, men who taught distrust of the divine and superhuman, men who never taught to their classes anything except technical facts, ignoring the entire subject of moral and religious experience?

"From the way He spoke, I gathered that moral and religious conditions at the university have greatly changed since the Bible was put out of the state schools."

"They have!" Dr. West spoke emphatically.

"And Jesus again seemed to know exactly what professorships came under His just condemnation. Man after man on the platform sat there pale and angry, but convicted in their own hearts of their neglect to use their great office as teachers to teach the student body the main thing, which, as Jesus said again and again, is righteousness.

"Never in all the history of the university have faculty and students ever heard such an address at the assembly. I do not believe any words can express the power of Jesus' appeal as He closed. It was a heart cry to the university to open the doors of the soul to God. Without in any way detracting from the value of the technical work the university is doing, He insisted that the main thing in education, which is and always must be religious development, righteousness, social democracy, love for God and others.

"I walked off the platform, with Jesus, leaving the audience, faculty, and students still seated in the hall. One of the teachers who came out and overtook us on the way to Mr. Maxwell's said it was a full minute before anyone stirred.

"Then the spell seemed to be broken, and the assembly broke up in a storm of feeling. What we saw out in the road a few minutes ago was probably student groups taking sides for and against Jesus. I have no doubt members of the faculty and of the fraternities are calling Him a 'boor' and a 'socialist' and an 'anarchist' and a vulgar 'sensationalist.' But no one can deny the fact that such an address, for sheer power and effect, was never heard at the university before."

"Do you feel that Jesus—ought—to have spoken as

He did?" Virginia asked it as if in her heart she was a little afraid.

"How should He speak?" Stanton answered in his deep voice, looking earnestly at Virginia as he spoke. "The usual talk at the assembly, I am told, is some refined, scholarly essay on some subject entirely removed from the great questions of conduct, of right and wrong, of pure and vulgar. What can we imagine Jesus talking about to students and teachers?"

"But—was He taking advantage of His invitation—to—to condemn the chancellor and the students and faculty? Will His action not make Him enemies?"

"No doubt. We shall probably have some illustration of it before the day is over. But did not Jesus make enemies among some kinds of people the minute He began His ministry when He was here before? Is He not the same in all the ages?"

Virginia looked troubled. Then her face cleared, and she said, smiling calmly: "I am willing to trust Him. He cannot do wrong. He must know best. But come, Uncle, come, Mr. Stanton. If we do not go down to the church, we cannot get in. I would not miss the meeting for the world. Let us start now."

"Maxwell will see to it that we get seats," said Dr. West. "But we had better go along. Looks as if there would be a crowd."

Accordingly they left the house at once. The moment they stepped out of doors, they felt that an air of excitement pervaded the town. The streets were filled with people, all hurrying toward the First Church.

As they joined the flow of walkers, every now and

then came to their ears the words that were destined to become oftenest spoken and heard all over the world, "Jesus is here!" uttered in tones of incredulity, amazement, passion, trust.

"Jesus is here!" Virginia murmured to herself in repetition of the words as they were repeated about her. She felt as if every day new vistas of life were being revealed to her, new visions of life's glory were about to reveal a new experience, and her heart was beginning to accept what life had to offer of new and mysterious unfolding—and ever and always at the center of all stood the reigning figure of Jesus.

What? Jesus was actually in Raymond? Living, talking, eating, sleeping, playing with the children, rebuking sin, encouraging righteousness, affirming the superhuman, declaring the fact of immortality, He Himself in the flesh manifesting the truth among them—

She walked along by the side of Mr. Stanton, silent but happy, eagerly anticipating this conference of Jesus with His own disciples.

Long before they reached the church, they began to realize what a crowd was gathering about it.

" 'And the multitudes thronged Him,' " murmured Stanton. It was with real difficulty they managed to get up to Mr. Maxwell's study door, to which Stanton had a key. The entire street in front of the church was blocked by the students and townsfolk clamoring to get in.

Mr. Maxwell had come over from his house with Jesus and He was lying down on the couch in Maxwell's study. At Mr. Maxwell's request, Stanton went out into the church room to see if all details of the seating of the

Jesus Is Here

congregation were being carried out. He came back into
the study to report that the church was packed. All the
ministers of all denominations were present and representatives of the churches' membership. Many of the
businessmen of Raymond had closed up their stores. Mr.
Maxwell's Brotherhood had managed the ushering
admirably. They had given admission to the ministers
and church members first of all, as the conference was to
deal especially with church problems. But an increasing
and fast-growing, restless crowd of people, including the
noisy and excited students, was outside, and as unreason-
able mobs are in the habit of doing, demanding admission in spite of the fact that the church could not hold
another person.

Maxwell came back from the couch where the figure
of Jesus was lying and said quietly to Stanton: "Go out in
front and tell the crowd He will speak to the people outside after the conference. Ask them to be as quiet and
patient as possible. Tell them this conference is called
especially for the church and should be respected."

Stanton immediately went out through the church to
the front of the building. As he made his way through the
aisles, he noted first of all the absolute quiet and hush of
the people. In spite of the enormous crowd that filled
every available space, there was no whispering, no restless
movement. It seemed to Stanton even in his brief passage
through the room that a Spirit was brooding over the
people, that even before He had appeared, the people in
the church were preparing their hearts to receive Him as
their Master.

One of the ushers helped Stanton push a front door

111

open and he managed to get out and face the mob. The people had poured up against the building, packing themselves in a living wall against the doors and sides of the church. Stanton's tall figure and deep but penetrating voice commanded attention, and his announcement of Jesus' appearance after the conference partly satisfied the crowd.

As he turned to go back into the church, Stanton noted different groups of men who seemed to be eagerly disputing, and he had a vague feeling of future trouble from these men, but could not have told what it might possibly be.

The moment he was back in the church and had gone down by the platform, he was entirely caught up in the wondrous experience of being in the same room with Jesus, actually listening to His matchless voice, fascinated with His personality, captured, soul and mind, by His look.

The seats on the pulpit platform had been arranged by Maxwell so that Stanton should have one of them, but he invited up some visiting pastor from a nearby town; and just before Jesus came out, he went down himself to a seat in a pew next to the front row. He did not notice until he was seated that Virginia was next to him. As he turned his face toward hers, Virginia smiled faintly, then a shy look of pleasure passed like a faintest gleam through her eyes; and then to each of them it seemed as if the very presence of Jesus as He came out into the church brought with it a new definition of life in all its deep mystery and endless beauty and power.

What was the impression of that first great church

conference held by Jesus? Long weeks after it was history, Stanton, reviewing it with Virginia, would come back to a few great facts.

First, there was the continued deep silence of the people, broken only now and then by an eager question.

After that, the pervasive calm of that Figure up there on the platform, so amazingly calm, so different from the splendid rage He had shown out at the university. It was a stupendous calm, unmatched for depth and confidence by anything they had ever seen.

Then there was that thrill of power and love for the church that every minister present felt with the first word spoken. What? The church was a power in the world? Yea, verily, the greatest of all. The gates of Hades shall not prevail against it. Nay, the power of Death shall be of no avail. The church is the institution He loved. It shall abide forever.

Through all the conference ran this deep pulsating note of exultant victory.

Stanton caught himself more than once wondering when the Figure up there would begin to denounce, to criticize, to call attention to the weaknesses and faults of ministers and people. What? No faultfinding? No criticism? No sharp exhortation?

The words of Martha on that memorable night occurred to Stanton and to Maxwell as the hour swiftly went by: "He comforted us."

Surely, the church needed that. Needed to be shown its greatness and its goodness. And He, the Master, the Christ, the Head of the church, was up there smiling, glad, triumphant, revealing to that gathering of tired, discouraged,

113

bewildered, and even self-satisfied pastors and people the grandeur of their call and the might of their heritage.

All this and much more passed into heart and mind. And at the close, in the deepening silence, while all hearts beat fast, what an appeal for union of life and labor on the part of all the different names of the church people! Always that appeal to the ministers and churches to come together somehow in His name. Would He not tell what was the first step? Aye: Love one another. That would prepare heart and mind for all other steps. But in the prayer that ended the conference, what winged angel was that speaking with matchless beauty in appeal to the Father?

And while the people were still seated with heads bowed and tears on faces long untouched by feeling, He passed through the aisle to go and take His message to the crowd whose impatient weariness could now be heard by those within. And as He went past him, Stanton was awed and stirred to the deep places of his strong nature when Jesus turned His look upon him, and then as He walked slowly through the church seemed to include in His loving glance every single person there. At that moment Stanton, as he afterward told Virginia, understood how Jesus' look could change a person's whole life.

It was impossible for the great congregation to go out by the front doors, owing to the immense crowd outside. The people slowly and for the most part silently went out of the side entrances, and a considerable number even left through Mr. Maxwell's study.

Mr. Stanton and Virginia went that way. As they were going out, they heard Mr. Maxwell exclaim as he turned to face a man just leaving through the study—

"Mr. Carter!"

"Yes. No doubt you are surprised to see me among the prophets." Carter spoke sarcastically. But his face betrayed unusual agitation.

"I didn't happen to see you," Maxwell said quietly.

"No. I took the liberty of getting a front seat with the rest of the pastors! That is the reason you overlooked me."

"Who was that man?" Stanton asked of Virginia as they made their way around to the front of the church.

"Mr. Jasper Carter, editor of the Raymond *Gazette*. I never saw him in church before. That is, not until last Sunday. He was here then."

"Did you notice his look?"

"Yes. It was the look of a man who is fighting some fear."

"Exactly." Stanton gave Virginia a glance of approval. "It was the same look on the face of the chancellor out at the university. It was fear and rage together. And with it all, he looked baffled, as if for the first time in his life he had come face to face with a person who knew him clear to the depth."

"Yes," said Virginia. "Have you not felt that true of Him in the little while He has been here—as if He had known us all our lives?"

"Yes," murmured Stanton. "He needs not that any should tell Him. 'He knows what is in man.' That to me is one of the greatest proofs that He is really Jesus."

When they had come out into the street, the mass of people was so dense that is was impossible for them to get very near the church. Mr. Maxwell and several of the pastors were near them. Jesus, as at the assembly, had requested that all formalities of introduction be omitted. More people were still coming to swell the crowd, and after Stanton and Virginia had come a little way into the edge of the circle already formed, in a few minutes it seemed to them they were forced farther into the multitude until they could see nothing in every direction but people.

And all eyes centered on the Figure up there on the top step by the front doors.

How marvelous that voice as it fell upon the ear of the farthest listener, compelling absolute attention! And what a message from Him who, as of old, looked upon the multitude with compassion because they were like sheep without a shepherd! Yea, even upon those who had come from idle curiosity, and those who already were beginning, like Jasper Carter, to hate and to fear Him! And to those who were indifferent and sunk in selfish ambition—to all of them He spoke with such commanding power that not a sound except His voice went out over the people, only the regular city sounds on other streets mingled now and then with the message He brought that day to the hearts of sinful, wayward, impure, greedy, hopeless men and women in that mixed multitude.

And then Stanton, his tall form towering up over nearly all around him, noted, with a look of anxious welfare for Virginia, as Jesus finished and calmly began to move down from where He had been standing, after gently asking the people to disperse, that the groups of men who had attracted his attention before the conference began as if with concerted movement to force their way up together toward Jesus. Cries arose. The multitude that had been standing there so long was now released from the strain and acting on nervous impulse might do any one of a number of things such as mobs do.

Still Stanton, shielding Virginia as much as he could from those who were beginning to surge back and forth around her, noted the figure of Jesus slowly moving down from the steps into the crowd.

Then suddenly right in front of him a woman started up with a great cry that for a moment drew all attention to her. She was holding up in her arms a blind child, a little girl. What was she crying out? Hush! Hush! What is she saying?

"Give her sight! Oh Jesus, open her eyes! It is not her fault! It is—"

Stanton could not hear the rest. Great confusion was about the person of Jesus. He had put out his hands, as if in deep compassion, on the child's head. Had he opened her eyes? Stanton could not tell. He had a dim glimpse of Maxwell and other ministers struggling to get nearer Jesus and crying out to the people to keep from violence. Even at that moment of fast-growing turbulence he was aware that dozens of press representatives with cameras were holding them up over their heads to get pictures, and then he found all his strength and coolness were needed to protect Virginia and himself from serious harm.

For the crowd had almost at once become an ungovernable mob. When afterward the facts were all told, it was proved that the student groups were not responsible for the things that happened there in front of the church that day. A few of the rougher, more dissipated sort, who had been enraged at what Jesus had said out at the assembly, had joined in the brutality of the hour, but for the most part the students courageously and with noble dignity defended Jesus from actual blows struck at Him as He tried to make His way through the dense and frightened, panic-smitten crowd.

Those who were chiefly responsible were groups of lawless men who had come in from neighboring towns, gatherings of ruffians who had for several days been prowling the streets of Raymond, attracted by the unusual excitement of Jesus' presence there—the same rabble that springs up suddenly in almost any manufacturing center on occasion of a wreck or a fire or a flood.

People surged back and forth without knowing why. Every moment increased the unreasoning uproar and violence. Groups of men fought with one another. When a man went down, others trampled on his body with reckless selfishness. A spirit of mad fear swept over the throng.

Richard Stanton thanked God in his heart for an athlete's strength. He had trained in lumber camps of Michigan and Wisconsin and had made iron sinews and muscles on board the mission fishing-boats of Labrador. And he needed every ounce of a splendid animal vitality now. Among the whirling of forms, fists striking, bodies hurled right and left, Virginia, bold of heart as she was and used in past years to brutal scenes in the Rectangle, was in deep peril. Stanton cleared a circle about her. It closed up again. By the use of tremendous strength, he defended her again and again from mad rushes that would have hurled her to the ground. He put his arm about her, and with one word and look she understood her great peril and his necessary act. Indeed, it is probably true that so fast had Virginia, during that tremendous week she had known Stanton, come along the path of her affection and feeling for Mr. Maxwell's assistant, that Stanton's protection at this unexpected crisis came like a culmination of weeks of acquaintance. At that moment it seemed to Virginia that she had known Stanton always. And as his arm encircled her and she felt his tremendous strength and courage exerted all for herself, a perfect thrill of pride and joy in him possessed her. Once he staggered and had almost fallen. She cried out and dragged at him with both hands. Blood was flowing over his face, and his coat had been torn off. The mob was fighting for its life regardless of anyone. Mad, infuriated, trampling, roaring, it swept up and down and around in great eddying circles of fury.

And then, when even Stanton with all his courage had despaired of safety for Virginia and himself, a Voice came over the multitude: resonant, commanding, musical, calm. It rose clear and distinct, deeply fascinating, seeming to catch up and enclose all the savage clamor and rage of the people.

It was the voice of Jesus. Stanton wiped the blood out of his eyes and looked. He stood near the place where the woman had held up the little blind girl. He was now holding the child in His own arms, and on His face was a look of perfect triumph as He spoke to the multitude.

And as Stanton looked in perfect amazement, he saw arms and fists that had been raised and striking suddenly dropped. The roar of the mob died away. The wild rushing of bodies was stilled. People glared at one another but no longer fought. What had the Voice said? Stanton tried to repeat it. What? "Peace! Be still!" Once He had said it when they waked Him out of His needed sleep in the little boat on the windswept waves of Galilee. Now He was saying it here. What? And the mob was awed and stilled! What manner of man is this that can quiet a senseless mob of infuriated men?

In the struggle of the past minutes Stanton and Virginia had been flung up within a few feet of Him. He looked out over the multitude and then smiled. Then He looked at Virginia and Stanton, and they felt in an instant that all love's mystery, all their seemingly mutual appeal to each other, so brief in time but so deep and eternal, were fully comprehended and approved by Him.

He turned, and with the child still in His arms, the mother following, Stanton and Virginia, Maxwell and a group of ministers, all bearing marks on their persons of the frightful scene through which they had passed, walked along to Maxwell's house through an opening quietly made for them by the people. They were dazed and smitten into silence. Never in all the experiences of their lives had they witnessed any such event. And it was only when Jesus had disappeared that the people began to disperse after seeing that those who were seriously injured had been properly cared for.

In all that wild madness, no one had been killed. People were asking themselves as they went back to their business or their homes, speaking in whispers, whether miraculous power had been exerted that day. Hearts beat fast at the memory of what they had seen and heard. And the excitement of the press representatives mounted every moment with increasing volume. What manner of person was this? They had come, most of them, to report a "story" of some fake. But what was the truth—

Stanton had parted from Virginia at Dr. West's. The doctor had remained at the scene of the mob to be of service to those who were injured. As Stanton, bloody, with torn clothing, a deep gash across his cheek, turned to go into the doctor's doorway, he smiled at the sight he imagined himself to look.

Virginia was almost as "presentable." Her hat had been torn off and lost. Her hair was all over her face and shoulders. Her clothing was rent, and someone in the mad whirl of arms and hands had smeared her face with a wide streak of dirt.

They looked seriously at each other a moment and then laughed. Out of the fullness of their hearts they laughed, not at each other, but together. If the sidewalk had not been crowded with people, what would they have said?

"I cannot thank you here," Virginia said hurriedly. "What do people say when their lives are saved?"

"I do not know," Stanton said in his deep, strong voice, softened to a whisper that lingered in Virginia's heart. "I wish I did. For you have given me life today."

Then, as if smitten with sudden fear, he who had the courage of all heroism left her and went up the path to the doctor's house. At the door he turned before going in and watched Virginia as she went up the street to her home four blocks from her uncle's.

She also had turned just an instant as he had, and each knew that across that distance, over the heads of the excited throngs that were passing, the perfect song of a perfect romance was being sung in their hearts. And each at the same moment was having the same thought that knit all of their new life up to that commanding, gracious, companionable, loving Person who in some mysterious but real way had been at the heart of their own thought of each other and always would be as long as love shall endure, which will be forever and ever.

That night Mr. Maxwell's house was besieged by representatives of the press. They clamored with increasing emphasis for admission. They all wanted to see this person calling Himself Jesus and get additions to their already exciting accounts of the day's happenings.

Henry Maxwell had refused admission to everyone. At nine o'clock that evening, the noise of the crowd and its demands became so insistent that Maxwell unlocked the front door and stepped out.

The newspapermen gathered up as close as they could get. Mr. Maxwell pleaded with them to withdraw.

"I can't let in one without all. Here are more than fifty of you. Besides, He is asleep."

"Asleep?" asked a representative of a big New York paper. "Do you mean to say this person called Jesus has to sleep at this time of day?"

"He has to sleep just like any other person. Consider, gentlemen, He has had a most tremendous day. He was exhausted when He reached my house after that mob. It would not be decent courtesy to disturb Him."

There was silence among the correspondents. Many of them were grown men, veterans in the newspaper world.

"But how are we going to get our stories?" asked a Chicago reporter.

"I don't know, gentlemen. But I do know that I will not waken Him now for all Chicago, New York, and San Francisco."

"Then give us a story yourself, Mr. Maxwell," said another, one of the older men.

"You must excuse me. I have not given out any interviews since—He came. I do not believe it is His wish. In fact, I know it is not. I shall respect it."

Another silence, broken by a man representing a prominent Washington paper: "At least tell us this one thing, Mr. Maxwell. Do you really believe that this person is Jesus?"

Mr. Maxwell was silent a minute. The newspapermen were crowded up together, evidently very eager to get his answer.

He spoke slowly and solemnly. "Gentlemen, I believe with all my soul and mind that the person asleep in my house tonight is Jesus Christ, the same person who lived on the earth before."

A deep and prolonged silence followed. Then several of the men began to ask more questions.

Mr. Maxwell courteously but firmly refused to say more and urged the men to leave the house, which they finally in good-natured unanimity agreed to do. As they left the door, Mr. Maxwell went back inside, while the newspapermen scattered to their hotel rooms, all deeply impressed with what they had seen and heard.

The New York man stopped suddenly and said to the Washington correspondent: "There! I meant to have questioned Maxwell about this camera story. I don't mind saying I have no picture."

"Nor I," replied the other quietly, but with deep excitement. "No one has. How do you account for that? It is unparalleled."

"I don't account for it."

They walked along talking with other groups that filled the hotel lobbies and swarmed over the town, roused into thrilling excitement over the day.

And somehow all over the city seemed to rise and swell in deep and widening intensity the awe-inspiring whisper, "Jesus is here! Jesus is here!" And everyone held their hearts in vague expectancy of the future.

At ten o'clock that night, Henry Maxwell, up in his study above the guest room where Jesus lay asleep, was summoned by the telephone. It was Stanton calling him.

"I cannot sleep. And I felt certain you must be awake. I want to inquire about—Him."

"He is fast asleep."

"How wonderful! What a stupendous series of events!"

"Yes. How little we could have dreamed it."

"Was the little girl that He carried given sight?"

A pause. Then—

"No. He gave her back to her mother, saying words I did not catch. And she went away apparently satisfied."

Another pause. Then Stanton's voice: "That cry to the mob! Was it not wonderful?"

"Yea. Indescribable. You were not seriously hurt?"

"No. A blow on my cheek."

"Miss Page took all bravely?"

"Yes. No one could have been braver."

Then Maxwell again: "I will tell you, Stanton, what I have told no one yet. He is going away tomorrow."

"Going away?"

"To New York. To Washington."

"But He has only just begun—"

"But do you realize Raymond is only one small place? He is eager to see the great multitudes and carry His great message elsewhere. Consider our blessing to have seen Him even once."

"Yea. But how can we live without Him?"

"He is with us always. Stanton, He said He wants to see you—and Virginia—before He goes."

A silence. Then from Stanton: "He is my Master, my Lord, and my God. I bless the day I saw His wondrous Light."

Before Mr. Maxwell went to bed, he gently opened the guest room door. The light was low in the hall, but a little of it entered the room.

The Guest was asleep, soundly. He breathed like a happy, healthy child. What wondrous scenes awaited Him in the great surging centers of population as He set His face from Raymond! Who could tell?

Mr. Maxwell closed the door, and in his own room, kneeling, he breathed a prayer, foreseeing in a waking vision some of the tremendous scenes through which his Master would soon pass. And as he fell asleep, there ran again and again through his heart as he thought of the Figure asleep in his own house: "Jesus is here! Jesus is here!"

SOMETHING TO THINK ABOUT

1. Why do you think Jesus made no mention of the alcohol and tobacco when He sat at the table in a social setting—and yet He later publicly denounced their abuse? Does this correspond with what we know of Jesus' behavior from the Gospels? What inferences can we draw about our own behavior when we are encountered with similar situations?

2. Sheldon makes a point in this chapter of stressing Jesus' humanity by telling repeatedly of His need for rest. Do you think this is an accurate presentation of Christ's nature? Why or why not?

3. In this chapter Jesus again fails to heal an innocent child. Jesus *is* here in our lives—and yet, just as Sheldon describes, He more often than not fails to heal those who seem to need His touch so desperately. Since His nature is surely still the same, why does Christ's presence among us today behave so differently from when He walked the earth two thousand years ago?

CHAPTER VII

It was a week after the great conference in the First Church at Raymond. Virginia had just come over to see Rachel, and as Rachel came into the sitting room with her boy, Frank, she exclaimed: "What have you been doing to grow so young and handsome? Stand right there, Virginia. What's the secret?"

Virginia stood still, facing her friend. Before her conversion to Christian discipleship, she had used her wealth and social influence simply for pleasure. Now, for the years she had dedicated herself to the service of her Master, none of her beauty had been lessened. But it had about it a more subtle loveliness and grace. And today as she came in, she was so radiant, so abundant in the splendor of her Christian womanhood that her friend could not refrain from comment. Virginia stood there in silence. There was a smile on her lips so gracious, so full of winsome life that it was irresistible. The little boy, Frank, ran up to her.

"Kiss me, Auntie Virginia," he said.

"Me too!" cried Rachel. She ran into Virginia's arms and the two friends laughed as the boy reached up his arms between them.

"I have come to tell you, dear. You shall be the first to know." And in few words she told her heart's secret.

"What! You! Virginia! Oh! I am so glad! And oh, how I shall enjoy having you for my minister's wife!"

"Rachel! How do you know— Besides, I shall not be your minister's wife. Only—"

"Only the 'assistant' minister's wife. But do you think I have been blind, or that a happy married woman like myself cannot see what has been going on when her dearest friend was concerned? Why, the very first night Mr. Stanton saw you, he was attracted to you."

"That is what he tells me," Virginia exclaimed. "And it helps us both a little to excuse the seemingly absurdly brief time we have known each other. Just think! Less than two weeks."

"But you are neither of you children, you know," said Rachel slyly. "Let's see. How old are you, Virginia?"

"I am thirty-four," said Virginia, smiling. "And Mr. Stanton is forty. So of course we, as you say, are not children."

"Do you call him Mr. Stanton?"

"I meant to have said—" Virginia paused shyly, almost as if Rachel were a man acquaintance. "To have said, 'Richard!' "

"That sounds better to me. How delightful!" And Rachel hugged her again. "God has been good to you, Virginia, in giving you the love of a real man."

"I know in my heart He has. For Richard saved my life there out in front of the church. And I believe, dear, I learned fully what he meant to me that day. And another thing I have not told you, the next day, the day Jesus went away, He talked with us and seemed to crown our love with the one great crown it needed."

Rachel was silent, looking at Virginia with deepest interest.

Virginia's face, happy, glowing with her newly found joy, was now wet with tears.

"Jesus spoke to us with a comfort and a joy we do not know how to express or explain. He had seen from the first time He met us how necessary we were to each other. And then Richard told Him that on the day of the riot, in the very midst of its confusion, or just as it was marvelously quieting under the astonishing command of Jesus, he knew, just as if Jesus had spoken, that He approved and commended and blessed our love for each other. Oh, we shall always carry with us all our lives His gracious benediction. Think of it, Rachel! We—Richard and I—have actually taken the hand of Jesus in the flesh and He Himself in person has actually blessed our love with His spoken word and His gracious smile. It does not seem possible."

"All of that astounding week seems impossible," said Rachel gravely. "But we know how real it has all been. I never could have borne the death of Eloise if Jesus had not been here." Rachel's tears fell, but they were not bitter, only the natural human tears of mother affection.

"Do you feel at any time as if Jesus ought to have brought her to life?"

"No. Not now. I have the greatest peace, Virginia, whenever I think of Eloise. Jesus gave me that peace."

There was a loving silence between the two friends while Virginia held Rachel's hand and caressed it. Then Rachel said brightly: "Have you told Mr. Maxwell?"

Virginia blushed and laughed. "No, but Richard is going to tell him today. We wanted to keep it to ourselves a while."

"Selfish creatures! Keeping it to yourselves at least a week! Virginia, I did not think you were so selfish!"

Virginia laughed again—a laugh that revealed her intense happiness.

"I am not going to apologize for the suddenness of it. I have no doubt people will be surprised. They will say it is not like me."

"Well, it is not like anything you have ever done yet. But don't you imagine anyone will be critical. I have not been so happy since Rollin, with my help, asked me to marry him. But—" and her face grew happily thoughtful— "what a blessing greater than mine or any friend's, dear Virginia, is the blessing He gave you both."

"Yes," Virginia said softly, her face glowing, her eyes looking afar. "Yes. We shall carry that gracious blessing of His all our lives. Thank God! Thank God!"

"Do you think we shall ever see Him again?"

"Not here in Raymond. He must go to as many other places as He can."

"Where will He go first?"

"To New York. Then to Washington. Then—He did not know Himself. But He bade us farewell, as if we should not see Him again here. I shall never forget His last words. 'Beloved, we shall all meet in the Father's House.'"

"It is what He said to Rollin and me at the grave that day. Virginia, how wonderful that we have seen and talked with Jesus."

"And that He has loved us and told us so. Oh, I am so happy! We want to serve Him all our lives and give our lives completely to Him."

After a silence, Virginia rose to go and Rachel asked: "When will you be married?"

"Very soon. We see no reason for waiting long."

"No. You have waited so long all these years it would be too bad to wait any longer!"

Virginia laughed, kissed Rachel and little Frank, and went away.

The boy turned to his mother and said: "Mamma, what makes Auntie Virgie so beautiful today?"

"Love, just love. It is the great beautifier of life."

"Is that what makes you so beautiful?"

"Bless you, my son, it must be," said Rachel as she clasped the boy to her heart and thought of Eloise and Rollin.

At about the same time in the day that Virginia was "confessing" to Rachel, Stanton was with Mr. Maxwell in his study at his house. They had been reviewing that wonderful week that would remain in their personal history as the most astonishing experience they would ever know on earth.

"What has been left as a result of His short stay with us?" Stanton was saying.

"The result? Stanton, it is simply overwhelming. I can understand now why it was not necessary for Jesus to live a long period of years on the earth in order to leave a deathless influence. Do you realize what courage and power the visit of Jesus put into the ministers? All over town yesterday everyone was talking about the wonderful sermons heard on Sunday. People said there was nothing like it in all church history in Raymond."

"I'm sure," Stanton said warmly, "we had a wonderful

sermon in our church. Mr. Maxwell, I want to say I never heard such a powerful sermon in all my life as you preached day before yesterday."

Mr. Maxwell's eyes glistened. He had already fallen in love with his great-hearted assistant, and his words of praise pleased him greatly.

"Thank you, Stanton, thank you. But what man could help preaching, after all we have seen and heard? The coming of Jesus and His message put such heart and hope into the church and into all Christian discipleship that it is not possible to measure its value. It will all lead shortly to a real and powerful union of the denominations in Raymond and all over the country. And that will mean a new and wonderful chapter in Christianity."

"But—how can we live without Him, Mr. Maxwell? In the short week He was with us—how we all learned to love Him! I would give anything right now to see and hear Him. What will befall Him in New York and Washington? How will He be received there?"

"It is impossible for us to say. I cannot help thinking of the quiet, unconcerned way in which He simply ignored the press representatives who had crowded into Raymond. And they hardly realize yet, that without in any way seeming to avoid them, He succeeded in foiling all their impertinent efforts to exploit Him for their own sensational purposes."

"It was the rarest possible exhibition of wisdom and calm indifference to publicity I ever saw," added Stanton. "Mr. Carter, especially, seemed to be disturbed greatly on account of Jesus' indifference to his paper and all attempts to interview him. Did you hear a rumor to the effect that

Mr. Carter was going on to New York to follow up His career there and expose Him if possible?"

"I have heard something of the sort, but I paid no attention to it. Carter is a violent egotistic man concerning all his ambition about his paper and its influence. I know he was deeply disappointed because neither he nor any of his reporters could get a picture of Jesus for his paper."

"Nor any of the other press representatives. Mr. Maxwell, do you put that down as a miracle?"

"I don't attempt to explain it. But my faith in Him after the first few doubtful hours seemed to me to rest on what He *was* rather than anything He *did*. His power and His sinlessness and His superiority impressed me irresistibly. I could not escape that for a moment."

Stanton was silent and both ministers seemed to be going over the great events through which they had passed. Then Stanton said gently: "Mr. Maxwell, I have a statement which I wish to make to you, not a confession exactly, and yet it is in one way—but—the fact is—I am planning to get married, to have that home you said a few days ago I ought to have."

Maxwell looked at his assistant keenly. "You're going to leave us? I don't know how I can spare you."

"I'm not planning to go yet, Mr. Maxwell. But I am planning to take from you one of your best—the best, I think, of your parishioners. All I can say is I can't help myself, and to tell the truth, don't want to."

Mr. Maxwell's face suddenly brightened up and he took a step nearer his assistant and put a hand on his shoulder. "Richard," he said in the affectionate manner that had knit him so closely to his own young people all the years, "I congratulate Miss Page and you. I don't know which one needs the other most. Let me call Mrs. Maxwell. She will be delighted. In fact we have once or twice actually wished this might happen."

He called to Mrs. Maxwell, and when she entered the study, he was about to break the news to her, but she smilingly anticipated her husband. "Oh I know all about it, Mr. Stanton! I couldn't be more delighted if Virginia were my own daughter. You have our heartiest blessing, Mr. Stanton."

Stanton's eyes glowed as he took Mr. and Mrs. Maxwell's hands. "I shall prize your friendship for her sake and my own." And then he added as Virginia had, "It was unspeakable joy to us to have Jesus speak to us as He did before He went away. That will follow us all our lives."

And then that silence fell between them—the silence that the world was to know more and more after its centuries of bustle and hurry and din, the silence that Jesus always brings—the peace that passeth understanding and is the source of more permanent power for righteousness than all noisy meetings and fussy "plans" for helping God do His work among men.

Stanton at last rose to go, but Maxwell asked him to wait a moment. "I want you to see something Martha has. Wait a moment."

He went out of the study and soon returned with Martha. Mrs. Maxwell had told him something of the girl's history, and Stanton was deeply interested in it. Besides, had not Martha been the first person to announce to them the advent of Jesus into Raymond and tell the story of His appearance at her church meeting?

Martha came in holding a little book in her hand. Maxwell asked her to show it to Stanton.

"Jesus gave it to me when He left the house," said Martha simply.

Stanton took the volume into his hands with a peculiar feeling of awe and opened it at the first page, which had a bookmark in it, and read: "Martha Lowell. From Jesus, her Friend." There was a date, and "Raymond."

Stanton gazed at the common inscription, fascinated. The volume was a New Testament, a small, flexible, leather-covered book.

"Why, this is priceless, Martha. Did you know it was priceless?"

"I know it is the most precious thing I possess," said Martha simply.

"How did He happen to give it to you?"

"I asked Him to write my name in my old Testament, and He wrote it with His own in this new one and gave it to me the morning He went away. Mr. Maxwell, do you think He will come back? Do you think we shall ever see Him again? I had such a comforting talk with Him that morning. You remember, Mrs. Maxwell, how He smiled when He stepped into the kitchen to say good-bye."

Neither Mr. Maxwell nor Stanton could avoid a feeling of surprise.

"But why not? Why not?" Stanton was murmuring. "What did we expect to see? A being so removed from common human things that He could have no feeling for human infirmities? No! No! We must overturn our old definition of God." He spoke aloud to Maxwell. "Have

135

you any such reminder as this?"

"No. Have you?"

"No. I would give anything if I had. Why did we not ask Him?"

Maxwell stared. "Yea, why didn't we? Martha was wise and now she is rich."

"He gave several of the men at the mission little books with His name. Mr. Grey asked for them."

"Grey was wise also," said Maxwell, smiling. "But I'm afraid, Martha, we shall never see Jesus in the flesh again unless we happen to go to New York or Washington while He is there. I am sure He will not return to Raymond."

"I shall remember Him forever. He is my Lord and my God," said Martha gravely, as she went back to her work.

"Mr. Maxwell," said Stanton, "did you ever wonder while Jesus was here about His—His—financial condition—did He have any money? Did that trouble you any, or—how could He buy books and travel and all that—"

Mr. and Mrs. Maxwell looked at each other significantly, and Mr. Maxwell answered: "He said one day, He had not come to satisfy curiosity about Himself, but to reveal the Father and His righteousness to the world."

"Thank God we have seen Him," said Stanton as he went away exalted in his whole being on account of his own transfiguring love for Virginia and the gracious, marvelous, personal touch of Jesus in it all.

On this same day in the forenoon, Jasper Carter sat in his office at the *Gazette* building. Barnes sat opposite him. On the faces of both men was a look of deep feeling and on Carter's it seemed near the point, every moment, of breaking out into one of his fits of characteristic anger and irritability.

"Nothing but a fake, a great big fake from beginning to end," Carter was saying as if he had already said it several times.

"Of course I don't agree with you, Mr. Carter," Barnes said very quietly. "But what is the use of arguing about it?"

"Arguing!" exclaimed Carter angrily. "Who is arguing! I am stating a fact. This person you call Jesus was a fake. What did He do while He was here?"

"He converted me, for one thing," said Barnes gently.

Carter started as if he had been struck.

"Well, I admit that was something unusual!" said Mr. Carter. "But name anything else He did."

Barnes did not offer to say anything.

"Name anything else!"

"I thought you just said you didn't want to argue about it."

"I don't. But name anything else this person you are so sure was Jesus did to prove His claim."

"Well," and Barnes's eyes began to flash with his old-time eagerness, tempered now by his newborn passion for his Master, "neither you nor the whole army of press representatives could secure a single photograph of Him. I call that something."

"A trick. It will be exposed sometime. But when He had a chance to do a real miracle, He failed. He couldn't raise Mrs. Page's child to life when He was asked."

"He would not."

137

"He did not. And did He heal any sick people while He was here?"

"I don't know. And if He had raised the child to life and healed every sick person in town, would you have believed in Him any more than you do now?"

"That is not the question!" Carter grew angry again. "If He is Jesus, He would have to do miracles."

"Mr. Carter, would you call that manuscript you asked me to read a literary miracle?"

Carter did not speak for a few moments. Then he exclaimed sullenly: "No! Just clever."

"Did you ever hear such a public speaker with such perfect command over an audience all the times you heard Him?"

Carter hesitated. Lying was not generally one of his faults. "No. I acknowledge I never heard His equal. But that would not make Him divine."

"But how about His stilling the riot in front of First Church? Do you think a mere man could have done a thing like that?"

"The crowd was exhausted. He waited for the psychological instant before He spoke. I don't see anything astonishing about it. What other proofs have you to offer of His being the Jesus of history?"

"I'm afraid I haven't any that would convince you, Mr. Carter, but I am fully satisfied about Him."

"Well, I'm not. He gave out that He was going to New York. A week has passed. He is not in New York, or if He is, no one has heard anything of Him. And in my opinion, it is the last we will hear, unless He turns up as an impostor elsewhere. Why should He go to New York or Washington? Do you know what would happen to the real Jesus if He were to appear in those cities?"

"I think the multitudes would greet Him and He would receive the greatest welcome ever given to a person."

"I don't. If He appeared in New York, the crowd would run after Him as they run after every new fad there, and then go back to their money-making. And if He appeared in Washington, the politicians and society leaders would express a mild surprise and perhaps go to hear Him if He condescended to speak in a fashionable hall and then go back to their receptions and amusements and forget Him."

"If Jesus appears in New York or Washington, people will not forget Him. Will the people of Raymond ever forget Him? Why, Mr. Carter, do you realize that new history has been made here by His visit? This is a changed town, due to His presence. I do not believe you understand what has happened."

Before Carter could reply, the Associated Press editor called him up.

"You said you wanted the first item from New York about—about—the person calling Himself Jesus."

"Well?"

"Here is an item."

"Go ahead with it."

" 'There is a rumor that the person purporting to be Jesus, who has recently startled the town of Raymond with sensational appearances, is in New York and may at any time appear before the public. So far, no definite location of Him has been made. It has been rumored that He is staying with a poor family in an obscure street. All attempts to find Him on the part of press representatives have failed.' "

"Is that all?"

"That's all."

Carter turned from the instrument and gave the message to Barnes.

"You see. Nothing but rumor. It was a fake. A very good one, but a fake, Barnes."

Barnes sat looking at Mr. Carter curiously. "Why are you so deeply interested in all this if it is only a fake, Mr. Carter? I have never seen you so profoundly stirred over anything."

Jasper Carter grew very red in the face. "I hate a sham! Christianity is a sham, built up on a tissue of lies about superstition and miracles and all that rot. I hate anyone who pretends to perpetuate all this sham, like this Jesus of yours."

"You hate Him because you are afraid of Him."

"I hate Him because He is a sham!" Carter shouted. "He would not dare appear in a city like New York or Washington before the thinking power of the nation. He knows—"

At that moment Carter was interrupted again by the Associated Press editor.

"An important news item from New York, Mr. Carter."

"All right. Go ahead."

" 'Jesus is here—' "

"Hold on. What's that?"

"I'm reading off the telegraph, Mr. Carter. Just as—"

"All right. Go on."

" 'Jesus is here! The most unprecedented event in the history of the world for the last two thousand years has occurred! At the conference of all the ministers and religious workers now being held in New York, suddenly there appeared the same person who created such a series of sensations in Raymond a week ago. There is no question whatever that it is Jesus. All the ministers present accept absolutely His claims and do not doubt His person.' There is a full list of well-known names here, Mr. Carter. Shall I give them?"

"No. Never mind about the rest."

Carter turned to Barnes. "Could you catch that?"

"Yes. Jesus has really appeared in New York and He is accepted as such."

"By the ministers. But not by the people generally."

"But all New York will pay Him honor."

"As long as He does not preach against the money god. Then they will crucify Him. How long do you think Wall Street would listen to Him, to say nothing of obeying His teaching?"

Barnes did not reply to this. After a while Carter continued: "Oh well, I haven't changed my mind. It's not the first time the world has been fooled. I may have to go to New York in a few days. If I do, I'll—"

"What?"

"I don't know," Carter spoke sullenly. "But if I get a chance, I'll expose the sham."

"Mr. Carter," Barnes spoke gently. "Why do you hate Him? Oh, I wish I knew how to tell you what a new definition of life I have had ever since I began to love Him."

For reply Carter turned his back on Barnes, and

141

Barnes went out of the office. On his way down to the reporters' room, he stopped in to see the telegraph editor.

Normally, the Associated Press man in the *Gazette* office was impervious to anything. News of all kinds from all over the world came to him first out of the fifty thousand in Raymond. Wars, murders, scandals, elections to office, assassinations of kings and presidents, upheavals in politics, floods, earthquakes, fires, world disasters of every sort—all this flowed into the little room to the telegraph editor and he clicked it off on his typewriter, piling it up for the news editor to choose from, imperturbable, unmoved, working like a machine himself. Everything was grist to his mill. Whether it was a world catastrophe engulfing thousands or the nomination of presidential candidates in a Republic, Hurd sat there coolly taking it off on his machine, a little more of a mechanism than his own typewriter.

But when Barnes went in, he found Hurd visibly excited.

"I say, Barnes, this is the biggest thing ever came off the wire. And there's just pages of it. New York has gone wild. In all my experience I never have taken anything like this. The New York papers are just swamped with it."

"Hurd," said Barnes, his eyes glistening with excitement and pride in his Master. "You were present in the mob last Wednesday. What was your impression of the way the crowd quieted down?"

Hurd turned squarely about and faced Barnes. "My impression? Barnes, let me tell you. I'm not an impressionable fellow, as you know. Who could be with all this human volcano spouting through him every day. But I want to say that when He—yes—I have to believe it is really Jesus—when He spoke those three words the other day, I seemed to feel a powerful hand put right on me and I just calmed down like a little child. I reckon I was one of the noisiest and most roughshod there. Fellows like me are, when we get going once. I tell you that was no mere man's work. No man living could have quelled that mob as He did."

Then, going back to his New York news, he continued: "Some astounding things are going to occur in New York. It does not take a prophet to say it. See here! 'Jesus has the unquestioning endorsement of all the ministers and church leaders. He has already spoken out in His first public utterance against the cowardice and selfishness of those who own and control the press of New York because they refuse to help civilization in its great battle against drink. The churches that are doing such great work without the aid of other forces are praised by Him and the ministers encouraged.'

"And look here! 'At the close of His first public day in New York, every minute filled with sensational events, He went home with one of the poor families on the East Side; but the papers cannot locate Him.' Won't that make the old man mad! I can't get over the stupendous way in which Jesus refused to be exploited by the press. The quiet calm, almost careless way in which He went His way while He was here, indifferent to the impertinence of those New York, Washington, and Chicago fellows, was the most astounding thing I ever witnessed. But—excuse my gab. Haven't talked so much since I was born."

Hurd shut up at once and continued his regular

occupation of rigid silence, but his unusual excitement communicated itself to Barnes as he went out on his way to the reporters' room.

"Jesus is here! Here in this world," he said to himself. "I have seen Him. Shaken hands with Him. He forgave me my sins personally! It is the one great event of my life! And He is going on with His mighty work! He has appeared to strengthen the faith of His disciples, to rebuke the hypocrites and the selfish, to comfort the broken-hearted and make people, even like Hurd and myself, feel the touch of the divine in our common lives! Thank God! Thank God! My Lord and my Savior!"

Barnes worked all that day with a tear in his eye and a heart throb of delight, and even as he worked, the vision of Jesus in New York, at the center of the republic's money fever, haunted him. He wondered every minute what Jesus would do there, how the people would receive Him, what would be the outcome of it all.

And then, suddenly, to the astonishment and disappointment and chagrin and wonderment of all disciples all over the country, He who had so thrilled every heart and roused to wondrous exaltation all minds that longed for Him, disappeared, leaving no trace; as if a drop of water had melted into the wide ocean. All New York was startled as much by His disappearance as by His coming. He had performed no miracles, had made no powerful impression except that one before the ministers. No one could be found who knew where He was or what His purpose could be. No one could say whether He would appear again, if at all. But hearts were heavy and hopes were quenched, hopes that had been kindled high by His first appearance. How could He disappoint the people? Where could He have gone? What was His future plan? Surely He would not vex the world by so imperfect and unfinished a task. He had as yet done nothing, except to show Himself to a few of His disciples. It was only a glimpse of heaven's glory! And the world was so hungry for a greater knowledge of His power, and it needed Him, Oh, it needed Him so much!

At the end of a month, there was still no sign of His presence anywhere.

Carter remarked to Barnes one evening as he was leaving the office, "How about this Jesus now? Do you still believe in Him?"

"I do," said Barnes bravely, but his heart was heavy. He had been anticipating wonderful events and he could not conceal his feelings. "I shall always believe in Him. I owe my new life to Him."

Carter eyed him closely. "Your new life? Well, but—my point was well taken, eh? It was a fake?"

"It was not. He will appear again."

"I doubt it. But never mind that, Barnes, I'm going to New York in two or three weeks to attend the national editorial convention, as you know. May be gone a week. Marks will be in charge here. If I see anything of your Jesus, I will wire."

He parted with Barnes, sneering in his rough fashion, and Barnes, whose Christian discipleship did not mean perfection yet, replied: "Mr. Carter, I may find it impossible to stay on the *Gazette*. I may have to leave while you are gone."

"You can leave any time," Carter retorted. "You may

145

remember I told you you could stay until I proved to you that the whole thing was a sham. Now that it is proved, I don't see why you have to quit."

To this Barnes made no answer, but he went home depressed and sorrowful, his heart heavy, grieving for the unaccountable silence of his Lord and Master. Where could He be? Why was He not overturning wickedness, comforting His disciples, inspiring the world with His presence as He had so wonderfully begun to do? Where was He? Surely His mission was not fulfilled in the appearances He had so far made.

Mr. Maxwell and Stanton were going over the same matter one day after a church meeting where many of the old pledge-takers had been present. The meeting had closed with many beseeching prayers that Jesus might return.

"He will, in His own good time I am sure," Maxwell had said. Stanton was also firm in his belief, as well as Powers and others. But the church workers could not account for His absence and silence.

Stanton lingered in the church study to consult with Mr. Maxwell about his approaching marriage to Virginia. "Of course we wish to avoid all just criticism of apparent haste. But Virginia is thirty-four. I am forty. We feel as though we have known each other always."

"My dear fellow, I am ready to perform the ceremony for you any time," Mr. Maxwell said smiling. "You need not fear any hostile criticism from Raymond people. They all love you and are really interested in your romance. I think it will disappoint many of them if you and Virginia don't get married soon."

146

Stanton laughed happily. He went over to see Virginia that evening, and two weeks from that same day was married, with a few of Virginia's old-time church and settlement friends present.

"You don't want to tell us where you are going with the two weeks' vacation the church granted you?" asked Mr. Maxwell after the ceremony, as he and the bride and groom were for a moment together.

Stanton looked at Virginia. "We are willing to tell you, aren't we, Mrs. Stanton?"

"Yes," Virginia said, out of her eyes shining the love light of perfect trust in her husband. "Mr. Maxwell ought to know."

"We are going to New York. We believe we shall see Jesus there. He consecrated and blessed our love for each other. Our hearts hunger for Him. We long to see Him again."

"God grant you may," Maxwell answered. "The Lord bless you both and give you a vision of Him. I do not, cannot, believe His mission is over."

Two days later Stanton and Virginia were in the great city.

For a week they had sought in various ways to trace some clue that would lead their steps to Him. But to no avail.

The eighth day, they were walking down Broadway and had stepped into Trinity Church. They had lingered there, enjoying the calm beauty of the interior, and on coming out, Stanton suggested a stroll down Wall Street.

They had hardly crossed Broadway, and Stanton, who was familiar with the city on account of his residence there when he was a social settlement worker, had directed Virginia's attention to the eight massive Doric columns of the United States subtreasury building prominent down the narrow street, when almost at once, as crowds gather in a big city, people seemed to spring up all about them, hurrying past them. Confused murmurs of disconnected but tremendously exciting talk rose about them.

Stanton, with Virginia eagerly clinging to his arm, suddenly exclaimed: "What was that! Someone said, 'Jesus is here!' "

He spoke to a fine-looking man who had just run out of one of the brokers' offices nearby.

"What is the excitement about?"

"Ah! I've only just caught the news. They say that Jesus has appeared again. Better follow the crowd. I have learned, sir, that crowds generally are pretty good signposts. They seem to know where the center of interest is."

All this spoken with great good humor but with an underlying deep earnestness.

Stanton and Virginia walked on with the man, each step drawing nearer to the front of the subtreasury building. Nearby, several city clocks struck the noon hour. The Trinity chimes sounded it. The narrow street was already black with people. Office doors opened all along and poured out a stream of men. Men were running in from Broad Street. Already the space in front of the treasury building was thick with people.

"Look!" Stanton suddenly spoke and pointed. "Look! Up there! By Washington's statue! There He is! He is there! Oh, it is true! Jesus is here! Thank God!"

"How do you know?" the man had asked, the man

who had answered Stanton's first question.

"I have seen Him. My wife and I have both seen Him. We are from Raymond."

"Ah! From Raymond, and you have seen Him? What do you suppose will happen now?"

But Stanton did not answer. He and Virginia could get no farther than the foot of the steps that led up to that gigantic figure of the first president. There the crowd completely hemmed them in. The street as far as eye could reach—men—almost all men. Virginia could see only here and there a woman. She seemed almost alone, surrounded by men who represented New York's material wealth, its selfishness, its material, gambling, crazy wealth —but interwoven in it also that indefinite energizing of forces that was not all self-seeking. But the money-loving men were at the heart of the greatest of cities, in front of a building representing in its structure patriotism and money—and up there at the base of the pedestal He stood. He was holding in His arms a little girl not three years old; the look on His face spelled command; the smile on His lips suggested infinite power and the strength that exercises it in love.

The little girl was looking up at Him, one hand resting, with perfect confidence, on Jesus' shoulder. In the other hand between her little fingers she held a small wreath of artificial flowers.

SOMETHING TO THINK ABOUT

1. Only Martha thought to ask Jesus for a gift. Do you think we, too, miss out on Christ's gifts because we fail to simply ask for them?

2. Have you ever experienced a time when Jesus' presence seemed to mysteriously disappear from your life, just as the characters in Sheldon's story experienced?

CHAPTER VIII

F our hours later Virginia and Stanton were in their room at the hotel. When they were seated, they looked at each other with glad but awestruck faces.

"What an astonishing scene!" Virginia was saying in a low tone. "Now we can understand a little better the great crowds that thronged Him when He was here before."

"Yes, and what tremendous power He had over all the people! Did you notice the people while He was talking?"

"No. I was too much fascinated watching Him and the little girl. It seemed to me we were standing at the very Judgment Day."

"Virginia, we were. It was a judgment day for New York and for every other money-loving, material-worshipping city. What He said and did must have burned into the heart and mind of every person there. Did you notice Jasper Carter?"

"No. Was he there?"

"Yes. And he bore the same look on his face we noticed the day of the mob. It was the look of a man who is afraid, and at the same time enraged, in the presence of a virtue and a sinlessness he cannot understand or beat down. I could not help thinking whenever I caught a glimpse of his face that the old Pharisees and scribes must have been like him."

"I did not see him," murmured Virginia thoughtfully.

"I was too much fascinated with Jesus. What a voice! What a message! What a compassion and what stern indignation against selfishness and wrong!"

"Men's faces went white when He lifted up the child. Ah! It was a sight not to be seen twice in an age. It will stay with us always. I am eager to write the account of it to Mr. Maxwell."

"And I to Rachel. Shall we do that now while our hearts are full of it?"

"Yes. It will be good for them in Raymond to hear of it. Of course the papers will have accounts. But we know how they so often exaggerate and color."

"Richard, do you think anyone could exaggerate that scene?"

"No. But of course I mean they could not grasp its full meaning. Neither can we. There were dozens of newspapermen there."

"Yes. Didn't you say there was an editorial convention here this week?"

"From all the states. This appearance of Jesus will be the event of their lives."

"And of ours, Richard. To think that He actually saw us and singled us out in the crowd and asked us to come to Him where He is staying this evening!"

"Yes. I understand and feel exactly the same. Virginia, Jesus has hallowed our love, and it will go always with us. Did He not appear at the beginning of His ministry at the wedding feast? Did it not teach the world His deep and tender interest in human love?"

Both Virginia and her husband began their letters at the same time. Stanton wrote with great rapidity as his

habit was and threw his great-hearted enthusiasm into his
vivid descriptions of that day's events.

[Letter from Rev. Richard Stanton, visiting in New York,
to Rev. Henry Maxwell, Raymond, describing the wonderful appearance of Jesus in Wall Street and its effect on
the city.]

My Dear Mr. Maxwell,

*Jesus is here! At last He has appeared in pub-
lic and begun what I believe will be a ministry of
power such as this great and wicked and good city
needs for its future.*

*The papers and telegraph will of course give
you details, but it was Virginia's and my good fortune to be at the scene in Wall Street today, and I
must write out of the fullness of my heart as an
eyewitness.*

*Virginia and I had been in Trinity Church
enjoying the quiet and the playing of the organ by
an old man who was rendering Guilmant's
"Evening Devotional." When we came out, we
started to walk through Wall Street but had not
gone half a block when the street seemed to fill
right up with men.*

*We could hear the cry on every side "Jesus is
here!" The crowds that poured out of the offices were
all sorts, but New York money was represented in
men who are worth their hundreds of millions, or
who at least control those fabulous amounts. I think
I have never seen a similar crowd of men anywhere.*

Virginia and a sprinkling of woman clerks and
stenographers were conspicuous in comparison.

Now, to understand what follows, I suppose
you ought to feel, as Virginia and I did, the exact
situation. There we stood at the center of what has
been reported as the money heart of the greatest city
of this republic. Things have been done by men in
this historic street that have ruined other men,
"deals" made in staggering sums of wealth, where
not one stroke of honest labor was involved, by
which men have "made" or "lost" fortunes. Men on
the prairies of Kansas and in the factories of New
England have had their entire personal histories
shaped and their lives beggared by the transactions
of men whose very names they have not known,
who have met in brokers' offices in this street and
"transacted" so-called "business" affairs, the object
of which has been to secure vast fortunes for themselves entirely regardless of what disaster might fall
on others. Here in this narrow street for years men
have gambled for money. The great god worshipped
here in this street is Money. Wall Street has been a
synonym all over the country for "speculation" and
"deals," and "control" and "financial jugglery" and
"greed" and "money getting" without any equiva-
lent being paid in the way of honest labor.

All this, of course, you know more or less, as
every American citizen knows in a more or less
exact fashion, but I doubt if anyone could feel it as
we did today standing right there in the very presence of it. The very word "money" seemed to cry

out in our ears from the buildings and the men,
and the very statue of Washington himself seemed
to possess some inscrutable knowledge of the many
selfish plans and money-loving schemes of this
street in which that mass of men stood, all facing
with sharp intensity the Figure up there by the
statue, holding the little girl in His arms.

How had He come there? Where had He
been in New York all this time during the weeks
that had elapsed since His first appearance at
the ministers' conference? No one could answer.
All anyone seemed to know was that He had
appeared at the noon hour holding the little girl
in His arms, standing there by the statue, calm,
silent, stern, waiting for the hearing that He
seemed to expect would be His, without any
previous announcement, with no herald to go
before, with no other irresistible attraction except
His own personality.

And like magic the street swarmed with men.
Before Virginia and I could reach the foot of the
steps leading up past the statue, the entire space
had almost been covered. We managed to get up
on the second step and there we were hemmed in
by the silent crowd.

After He began to speak, absolute silence
prevailed.

The little girl looked like an Italian. She had
one hand on Jesus' shoulder, the other was holding
a little wreath of forget-me-nots such as are
frequently seen in the ten-cent stores.

When Jesus began to speak, He instantly commanded attention on account of His quiet but amazing knowledge of the most intricate "transactions" on the street. I saw man after man glance at his neighbor with stupefied wonder as Jesus in a few short clear sentences revealed the very inner dealing of the speculative heart of America.

And then before anyone could tell where the transition had taken place, He was talking about the little girl and her artificial flowers.

These flowers, He said, were made in a tenement room, and He named the street where the tenement stood and then gave the owner's name. The little girl by working all day could make 540 of these flowers, for which she was paid 5 cents. A list of figures, quietly given, as to the profit made by the dealers of these flowers, followed.

And then, the whole Figure of the Man seemed to undergo a marvelous change. He grew suddenly taller and larger. His voice rang out over that mass of money getters like a trumpet of God. It seemed to me as I listened that He was speaking to all New York. And He was. The men around Him, their faces blanched with fear and self-condemnation, represented money worshipping New York in its entirety. The little girl whom He passionately held up high for them to gaze upon, represented humanity, worth more in her little self than all the money in the city, worth more than the city itself, worth more than the entire world. And yet she was being exploited in order that men

156

who already had millions might grasp millions more. She represented the greed which lay like a canker at the heart of a country's financial scheme, which trampled on worn-out women and defenseless children to keep up its luxuries and indulge in its selfish habits regardless of the precious humanity it trod into the grave.

That voice of Jesus! How tender, and how stern! Tender to sinful women and little children! Stern to scribes and Pharisees and hypocrites, no matter in what age of the world they live. I could not help thinking, as I listened to its fascinating strength, of other times when in Palestine He must have astonished wonderful mixed audiences of Roman soldiers, Greek philosophers, Jews, Asiatics, Africans, traveling merchants from various lands—the miscellaneous horde of all languages and pursuits that gathered in Jerusalem, who must on more than one great occasion have fallen under the indescribable charm of His words.

What a picture I could have secured there if I had been capable of placing that scene on canvas! I do not know how long He spoke, and I could not give His language in all its detail. I saw one newspaperman begin to take notes and then he stopped. His eyes gazed at the speaker—he resumed his note taking and stopped again. And then, as if completely under the spell of the voice, he simply listened—like all the rest, his professional duty as a reporter swept aside in the presence of such a tremendous tide of righteous wrath, that even I myself, innocent as I was of all the injustice He was rebuking, crouched and cowered as if I had been guilty.

I do not know how long He spoke. Somehow, as we learned during that blessed week at Raymond, time, when one is with Him, goes by unreckoned.

But when He paused, a silence brooded over that crowd so deep and painful that it was almost with a throb of relief that a cry was heard, a human cry that rose over the heads of the multitude like a lost soul's last wail of remorse, a cry so full of anguish and repentance that even while it broke the silence that was unbearable, it added another and different note of strangeness to all the astounding scene, and men's hearts stopped and then throbbed fast again as a man, holding his arms high up, was seen struggling to get nearer Him.

And the cry that rang from his lips was spoken with deepest passion.

"God be merciful to me, a sinner! God be merciful to me, a sinner!"

The crowd gave way for him. And he struggled up until he reached Jesus' feet. He fell down on the steps then, and we could see Jesus stoop and raise him.

Then a man near us, who had been with us when we entered the street, spoke out but under his breath—

"What! Clay Ross!"

"Who?" I asked.

"Clay Ross. Of the Westgate Securities Company."

Another man spoke. "He's the real purchasing agent and owner of this child-labor material. What's that? He can't be—"

Numbers of voices were raised. The deep spell of the Master's appeal was broken. I found myself looking at Virginia as if I had been somewhere else and had suddenly come back. Virginia was looking at me in the same way.

Men began to move. No one had stirred a finger all that time. We could see Jesus talking with the man who had cried out.

And then He began to descend the steps, still holding the child, and with one arm over the shoulder of the man who came along beside Him, the man's eyes lowered, his whole bearing like that of one who had met with a mighty experience. And no one could interpret his look.

The crowd gave way as Jesus came, silent and apparently oblivious of the multitude. But as He was passing Virginia and me, He paused and, in a tone that I am sure none heard but ourselves, asked us to come and see Him tonight.

Then we saw Jesus passing slowly through the multitude, the man who had cried out going with Him, until, together, Jesus, the little girl, and the man passed down the street and out of our sight.

Slowly the great crowd dissolved. It was noticeable how subdued men's voices were, how deeply smitten they had been in heart and mind. Somehow I could not help asking myself whether the "transactions" in Wall Street that afternoon would be just the same as they had been through the years.

It has not been easy to describe what the effect was of His presence and His message. I have been able to convey to you only a hint of what it all was.

We are anticipating with keenest interest our meeting with Him tonight. No one in New York has known of His address. We gather from the address He gave us it must be in the great East Side tenement district.

The scene this afternoon must be only the beginning of gigantic events to follow. Everyone seemed to feel the premonition of it. Hundreds of men in that gathering this afternoon must have been stirred to deepest anger, if they were not, like this Clay Ross, convicted of deepest selfishness and heart sin. And when once one begins to hate Jesus, history shows that to be as deep and relentless a passion as when love for Him makes one ready to die for Him. To what will it all tend? Money-loving New York will not endure even Jesus, if His teaching shall tend to the destruction of its old-time principles of money-getting. But it may be, after all these years of Christianity, there is enough leaven in the lump, even here, to change and reconstruct financial society and rebuild it on the foundation of brotherhood. The most fundamental *things will follow what Jesus may do within the next few days.*

Perhaps He will—but we speculate on His future plans. Only we know all things are in His hands, and the world He came to redeem so long ago will be redeemed by Him; of that we feel certain.

You may look for another letter tomorrow after our visit with Him tonight. It seems incredible—it is—to think of our actually going to see Jesus in the flesh.

We both send love to you, in Jesus' blessed name.

Affectionately,
Richard Stanton.

The morning following the Stantons' visit to Jesus, they both wrote again of their experiences. Virginia's letter to Rachel will perhaps even better than her husband's describe the remarkable evening they spent with Jesus in the East Side tenement.

[Letter from Mrs. Richard Stanton to her old friend Mrs. Rollin Page after an interview with Jesus in New York on the evening following the now historic scene in Wall Street.]

Dear Rachel,
I do not know whether I can in any real way describe the visit Richard and I had with Jesus last night following the great scene in Wall Street

about which I wrote you yesterday. It is all so amazing—this meeting with Him—that we seem to be living in a dream.

Only, as I read the papers this morning, I realize how wonderful a fact it all is. All New York is stirred to its depths. Everyone acknowledges that this person is Jesus. The Times *declares His presence to be the greatest event historically in all the world's history. The* Tribune *can find no parallel to His appearance and says no one can predict the tremendous changes that may be made due to His presence and preaching. The* World *declares His message yesterday in Wall Street was revolutionary and may lead to the most fundamental upheavals in financial methods. The* Sun *in an editorial that covers the front page announces a new standard of life has appeared, or rather a new emphasis on the old standard, and predicts any number of radical redemptive forces to be set at work.*

The main thing, of course, is that everyone acknowledges Him to be Jesus. There is no questioning of His person or His power.

The newspapermen have reason to feel awed at His power. So far not one paper has been able to secure a picture. Attempts have been made to draw sketches. Some of them are printed in the morning papers. They are all a failure, by the consent of the newspapers themselves.

Other wonderful things are a part of all this, but to the mind of Richard and myself, nothing is so great about Him as Himself.

How can we describe that? We can only say what we actually witnessed and felt. When we reached the place of His abode, following the address He gave us yesterday, we found it was the poorest and worst tenement block in the city. We went up five flights of stairs and knocked at a door at the very end of a dark passage, and Jesus Himself opened for us.

When we went in, at first we could not distinguish anything clearly. But the first person we recognized was the man who had cried out, "God be merciful to me a sinner!"

And what do you think he was doing?

He was seated at a small table by the side of the little Italian girl Jesus had held in His arms there by Washington's statue, actually trying to make artificial flowers like those the little girl had held in her hand while Jesus was talking!

I think we were so astounded at the sight that at first it absorbed all our thought. Then we began to note other things in the room.

There were at least nine other persons there beside the Master. And they were all at work making various articles of clothing or wreaths similar to those in the child's hand. There were five children, from three to nine years of age, two women and two men.

The room was about ten by twelve in size. Opening from it was another room without any window, in which we could see two other women using a sewing machine. There was a small stove

163

in this room. Over it hung a series of lines from which hung doll's dresses. A pot of glue was on the stove close by the side of a kettle, which we learned afterward contained some vegetable soup.

Both rooms were crowded with paper boxes that contained the crude materials brought in, out of which flowers and doll clothes were being made.

I have been familiar, as you know, Rachel, with slum conditions in the Rectangle, for a good many years. But there was something about the conditions here in these two rooms where these human beings herded together that was desolate and hopeless in the extreme. It seemed to be absolutely beyond redemption even by God Himself.

And then I felt dazed in mind and heart as I looked at Jesus and saw Him actually living among these creatures.

He preserved the same all-pervading calm He always shows. That, so far, is His most command-ing quality. Even at the height of His indignant denunciation in Wall Street, I could not escape that feeling of calm in the midst of the torrent that swept through Him.

He went from one to another, quietly helping in the work, a little after we came in. And after we had been there perhaps an hour, though we kept no account of time, He cleared away a little space on one side of the room, and going to a cupboard, took out some dishes and set them on a table.

Then He went into the other room, and we

could hear Him gently speak to someone there,
who we afterward learned was sick, lying on a
mattress on the floor.

Then He set the soup and small plate of bread
on the table and with a smile, such a smile as only
His face could reveal, He motioned all to stop
their work and eat.

We sat at the table with the rest. Jesus held
the little girl in His lap. She was so tired that in a
few minutes she fell asleep with a crust of the
bread between her lips.

But when all were seated, He lifted His hand,
and in the language they understood, He asked the
Father's blessing.

There was a moment then, Rachel, when I
felt my heart almost breaking. Here sat the Jesus of
the centuries; He who overcame death and hell;
He who raised the dead and forgave sins; He who
was one with the Father. Here He sat amid these
sordid, poverty-smitten humans, accepting their
condition, helpless to relieve it—and only half an
hour's ride from where He sat were Dives and his
tribe surfeited in luxuries, waited on by swarms of
servants, going to sleep in clean and perfumed
chambers—and—

Then I would begin to get some faint glimmer
of His mighty purpose in being there among these
people, and to see dimly why He did not by some
stroke of divine power smite the system under
which we live with some sudden catastrophe as a
rebuke for its injustice and cruelty.

During the meal Jesus spoke naturally and helpfully to all. And after everything had been eaten in eager haste, as if the time were precious, all went back to work again while Jesus put the little girl on a couch and Richard and myself removed the dishes, washed them, and put them away.

Just as we finished this work, which Jesus smilingly allowed us to share with Him, the door was violently burst open and a drunken man came in.

He trod on the paper boxes as he lurched over the floor, and going up to the table where the man, Clay Ross, was at work, snatched a nearly finished wreath out of his fingers and tore it in pieces. He then reached out two filthy hands and crushed between them a large number of artificial blossoms.

Richard had made strides toward the man to stop him, when I saw Jesus lay a hand gently on his arm, and Richard drew back.

The drunken man went up to one of the women and struck her over the head and shoulders several drunken blows. The woman uttered feeble cries, and one of the other men tried to protect her, swearing horribly all the time.

The drunken man seized a chair and lifted as if to fling it at the man. At this moment the little girl awoke, sat up, and began to cry.

Then the drunkard turned as if in fury toward that part of the room and my heart sank in fear and amazement as I saw him fling the chair over toward the child and then stumble toward her, while Jesus stood there silent, calm, motionless. He who had driven the traders out of the temple, He who had stilled the angry waters, He who had braved the soldiers sent to arrest Him so that in fear they all fell backward, was standing there allowing this drunken brute to harm, perhaps to kill, this little child for whom He Himself had pleaded that very day.

It was incredible! I could not believe it.

The drunkard kicked the child twice. She screamed and covered her face with her hands. The sick woman in the other room came running in and fell down in front of the child, kneeling and holding up beseeching hands to the drunken father. And still Jesus stood silent and motionless and my heart almost stopped in its fear and trouble and I noted Richard's powerful fist knotted and tense, as his look besought the Master for permission to throw the brute out of the room, and still Jesus made no sign.

The man struck the woman a cruel blow across the face and a red welt sprang up and a stream of blood began to trickle over the woman's cheek. He raised his arm again as the woman sank fainting at his feet. I felt I could bear no more, when suddenly the man, Clay Ross, arose, knocking over his chair as he got up.

With one stride he was on the drunken man and the blow the latter aimed at the woman fell *on Ross's own head. He seized the man, pinioning his arms to his side and with much exertion, as if his physical strength were not great, he managed to drag the drunkard across the floor back from the woman. The man resisted with drunken fury. But as the two struggled, trampling over the boxes, which now were scattered all about the room, the drunken man stumbled over something, loosening the other's hold as he fell heavily.*

Clay Ross wiped the sweat from his face, looked around as if dazed and confused, and then went over, picked up the chair he had overturned, and sitting down, put his elbows on the table and sobbed like a child.

Then Jesus raised the sick woman, and with my help and Richard's, we carried her back into the other room and laid her down on her mattress.

And now, Rachel, you will have to take this next statement just as I have to make it and believe me to be describing exactly what I saw.

We know that Jesus did not save Eloise when she was ill and did not exercise His power to bring her to life. And we know your heart is satisfied that He did the best for you.

But as we laid the woman down, apparently lifeless—although I could not say she was—I saw Jesus bend over her and whisper something. With a look of compassion that not even an angel of heaven could equal, He seemed to be asking this beaten, brutalized mother and wife a question. Was it a question that His whisper carried across that mysterious silence which Death creates for all of us? I do not know. But I do know what I saw.

Jesus wiped the blood from her face. He put His hand on her head. She smiled, then opened her eyes and sighed. Then she looked calmly and gladly at Jesus, and I saw her raise His hand to her lips.

Then Jesus smiled, but lifted His finger as if in caution. The woman closed her eyes again, breathed like a tired child, and fell asleep.

We went out of the room, and I saw Jesus take the little girl and, sitting down by the couch, He sang a soothing song.

Such a song, Rachel! No one can ever copy that! But if the child was hurt, she did not complain. She smiled up at Jesus and once raised her hand and caressed His face. And He smiled back and sang His song. Where had He learned it? Oh, Rachel, I feel afraid and astounded when I think of all these things.

While all this was happening, the man, Clay Ross, had lifted up his head and was talking to Richard. Evidently Richard had spoken to him and told him a little about who we were and why we were present.

As I sat down near them, I noticed that the workers on the wreaths and doll dresses were at work again, as if nothing had happened out of the ordinary for them.

One of the men had gone over to where the drunken man still lay and dragged him like a bag of old clothes, over into a corner, protesting all the time at the ruin and loss occasioned by the breaking of the paper boxes and the destruction of the material.

But when I had come over to Richard, I was fascinated by what Clay Ross was saying.

"Clay Ross!" Do you recognize, Rachel, the name of one of New York's most noted promoters and contractors of labor?

What was he saying? It was incredible, but the truest thing he ever said.

"Mr. Stanton, this day marks a miracle in my life. When I went out into the street this afternoon to see and hear—Him—I had no other motive but idle curiosity, just like every other broker and speculator there. But from the moment He began to speak, I knew in my heart that something great was going to happen to me. I have lived for forty-five years the regular life of a professional money-getter. Money has been my God. I am a type of hundreds and thousands in this town. I lived, ate, drank, dreamed, loved—money.

"In among all my other schemes, I have for years been at the head of the contracting firms that supply the material used in nearly all the sweat shops and child labor contracts. In addition to all the rest, I have all my life been one of those respectable rich men in New York, who has believed in the brewery and the saloon and I have always voted to license the saloon, saying what thousands of men in New York say, that it is here to stay and it is the only sensible thing to do, and *so forth. I have always had liquor in my home and at my club and own heavy shares in brewing concerns and all that.*

"You saw what happened to me today? If I were to talk all night, it would not add to what you see and I feel.

"For the first time in my life, I am living. Jesus is my Redeemer. I know my sins are forgiven. I have been a very wicked, selfish, sinful man. In New York money circles I have passed for a good financier, a successful businessman, a respected citizen. In reality, as Jesus laid bare my life as He talked, I am convicted of being a man guilty of nearly every crime against my brothers and sisters and against my own life.

"I would die for Him. When He put His arm around me there today, I felt ready to follow Him to the end of the world. I understand now how a man would leave his business as Matthew did and follow Him.

"I was never happy before—never knew what real happiness was. Now I know. If He will tell me how, I will give the rest of my life to humanity.

"Do you know why He stood there a few minutes ago and looked on while that drunken brute beat up his family? It was to let me see and feel the horror of the thing I have all my life been so 'respectably' defending. And when I got up and put my hands on that drunken representative of the wealthy brewer, I did the first real thing in all my life that sprang out of an honest personal

conviction.

" 'Friends' (and he said it in a tone I cannot convey), 'I am a new man in Christ Jesus. Once I was blind. Now I see. I will follow Him wherever He leads me.' "

Before we came away from that place, Jesus frankly and with perfect comradeship revealed to us His plans. He will stay in New York some time. He will appear again to the ministers and encourage and help them. He will bring His message and His helpfulness to many places. He will strengthen the faith of His disciples.

And then He plans to go to Washington. And then—you remember the United Congress of World Christianity is to gather here in New York next fall. He will be here then! What more fitting than that He of all persons should be present and speak as never man spake!

Great events are coming. How wonderful that we should be privileged to live at a time like this! Now I understand what it must have meant to him who wrote that he testified of what he had "seen and heard."

Richard and I have "seen and heard" Jesus, and our hearts are aglow. Our picture of Him as we last saw Him there last night, is this:

He spoke to us as He sat there holding the child, blessing our human love for each other, speaking with such whole-hearted affection for us, that we could not help weeping for joy as He spoke. And then He raised his hand in benediction

over us and the child and over the sordid room,
full of dirty, sinful, common humanity, letting His
hand fall with a gesture that even included the
drunken wretch on the floor; and we understood
as we stumbled down the filthy stairs, a little of
His reason for living there; we caught some
glimpse, a little perhaps, of His divine sharing
with human suffering, and we came away with
our hearts throbbing at the thought of His human
affection. I wonder, Rachel, if we shall ever see
Him again! We must start for Raymond tomorrow,
as our little vacation is over. But if we do not,
nothing can ever take from us the blessed experi-
ence of our personal meeting with Him. It is
woven into our very heart history; it is a part of
our eternal love for each other.

Your sister in Christ,
Virginia Stanton.

By the time Stanton and Virginia had reached Raymond, the whole world was talking and reading about Jesus and His appearances. In New York there was not even a hint of any doubt as to His personality or power. But the general public was in a constant fever of expectation, wondering at His next appearance and daily asking one another questions concerning Him.

The churches and ministers were electrified by His coming. Never had there been such powerful preaching as since the time of His first message. Pulpit and pew demanded in His name that tremendous evils like the saloon be removed from the life of the city. Day by day the agitation grew for a more brotherly rule of financial life. The very Spirit of the Master seemed to be on the streets, and people's hearts throbbed with new passion with every dawn, as they awoke and said to themselves, "Jesus is here!"

The friends in Raymond were in some ways even more excited over it all than the people in the big city. They had already felt the touch of His life, and they followed every movement of His plans through the New York press. So it was with no ordinary curiosity that Mr. Maxwell opened his New York newspaper four days after Stanton's return and read the following, written evidently at white heat by an eyewitness of an event that followed closely on the Wall Street incident, about which, according to the writer, people were still talking with no abatement of interest and wonder.

Mr. Maxwell read aloud to Stanton and Virginia and Rachel and Rollin, who had stepped into the study that morning to talk over Rectangle matters.

" 'The appearances of Jesus in the city have been without a parallel in history, except possibly His own. There is no question He is what He claims to be. Since the place in the East Side tenement where He has been staying has been discovered, He has come into the city and is openly and boldly working and preaching in the churches.

" 'He has created even in this short time the most intense and enthusiastic devotion among the ministers and churches. All denominations are flocking around Him. It seems probable that a new chapter in interchurch union will result from His presence and a working plan grow out of His counsel that will tremendously increase the power and influence of His disciples.

"'His preaching is indescribable in its beauty, its power, its persuasiveness, its appeal, its singular simplicity, its captivating charm. All ages, classes, parties, nationalities feel its winsomeness. He does not scourge the church nor call attention to its weaknesses. He speaks with transcendent power of its mighty history, its unparalleled achievements, its sacrificial martyrdom. The effect is irresistible. There is no question He is giving the church and the ministry such a marvelous vision of their opportunities that they are preparing to enact again the triumphs of the great centuries of Christian conquest. What the results will be for Christianity no one can predict; but it is safe to say they will be something very remarkable.

"'He is a tireless worker and speaker. With all, He is the calmest and most serene public person the people have ever known.

"'Those who are nearest to Him say that at the close of His day's ministrations He appears exhausted and sleeps the deep and dreamless sleep of childhood.

"'Every one of His appearances is the scene of tremendous demonstrations. Whenever He is recognized on the streets or at public gatherings, the people begin to say 'Jesus is here!' and He is the center of instant attention and attraction. There are times, however, when He seems to move unnoticed among the people, like any average man.

"'His voice is of matchless volume and glorious in its reach of tone and His smile is marvelous in its attractiveness. Still, no one has yet satisfactorily described His appearance.'"

Mr. Maxwell paused and looked up. His listeners

returned his look. "The same as when He was here," said Mr. Maxwell.

"At the same time"—Virginia spoke eagerly—"we shall never forget how He looks."

"To the end of the world," said Stanton gravely.

Mr. Maxwell went on reading:

" 'Last night the most fashionable and most widely advertised event of the season in theatrical circles took place. Avonarina and her chorus of dancers were to render the famous scenes in "The Girdle of Venus."

" 'Opinions have differed concerning the presentation. Avonarina's art is in some respects beyond criticism. Concerning her own power to attract—we may almost say ensnare—there is no question.

" 'Never in all the history of New York's theatrical inducements has such a throng filled the opera house. Never have the displays of wealth been so lavish or the outpouring of visible and physical adornment been so enormous and extravagant. And never has Avonarina appeared to such superb advantage.

" 'The first act had been fully completed. Avonarina had appeared, called repeatedly by well-nigh frenzied burst of applause before the curtain, which had finally risen for the triumphant initial entry of the "Venus Pageant," when to the astounding of everyone in the house, a cry suddenly arose, "Jesus is here!"

" 'The cry rang through the house like a trumpet. There in the center of the house He stood. Those who were nearest to Him said afterward that His eyes shot lightning and His voice swept up and over the audience like a sheet of audible flame as He spoke.' "

SOMETHING TO THINK ABOUT

1. Virginia writes in her letter to Rachel, "Nothing is so great about Him as Himself." Today, what distracts Christians from the Person of Jesus? What do we focus on rather than simply Himself?

2. While Jesus speaks with anger and power against those in power, He is quiet and gentle in the midst of drunken violence. Why do you suppose His attitude is so different in the two settings?

3. In Sheldon's story, Jesus so far has spoken out against child labor and poor working conditions and the saloon industry. If He were to visit our world today, what do you think He would openly condemn?

4. As Christians, we believe Jesus *is* present in our world today. What would need to happen if the rest of the world were to recognize His presence in places like Wall Street and other centers of commerce?

CHAPTER IX

M r. Maxwell paused in his reading for another instant.

"You remember, Stanton, the talk we had with Jesus one evening about the amusements of the people?"

"Yes, and the splendid reply He gave to our questions. The whole attitude of His heart and mind was absolutely clear and wholesome as, of course, we knew it must be."

"As it was on every question we put to Him. And so we are perfectly prepared now for His attitude in the face of this dissolute and demoralizing woman and her company. But what a tremendous scene it must have made."

"Yes—yes. Go on, Mr. Maxwell," cried Virginia and the others. "We cannot wait to hear the rest."

Mr. Maxwell resumed his reading—

" 'We have already spoken of the wonderful tone of Jesus' voice. It was remembered after the great excitement of the evening was over a little that He had begun to speak just as the people on the stage had struck the first note of the voluptuous strain of the "Pageant." The opening note is a loud full staccato. But over and through and beneath and around, the voice of Jesus rang through the house, so clear, so strong, so imperious, that it smote ear and mind and heart like a physical blow.

" 'He stood there in the center of the orchestra seats after that first utterance and there was a deathlike silence, so prolonged, and faced with such absolute calmness on His part that the effect was actually terrifying.

" 'Then He began to speak in such a low quiet tone that the deep silence was still unbroken. The people on the stage remained in their places. No one moved. Avonarina, in the front of the group, seemed smitten with curiosity, simply, at first, but as He went on, the Voice stronger and more and more striking, she was seen to cower down until at last she actually crouched upon the stage on her knees.

" 'We have already spoken of the difference of opinion concerning the motive of "The Girdle of Venus." It has been permitted on the stage of New York as an artistic production crowned by Avonarina's genius. In reality, it is no more than strict candor to confess that portions of this production contain scenes and dialogues that are not just the thing for self-respecting people to see and hear. * Among those present were many "leaders" of society and a large number of church people.

The description of a recent theatrical production put on the stage of a large theater in an eastern city contained exactly the language quoted above. At the conclusion of the article the newspaper critic added that not a single person expressed his disapproval by leaving the house.

" 'The denunciation of the Pageant that now fell from the lips of Jesus was terrific in its severity. He condemned the motive and the presentation of it with scathing words that unsparingly included all those who supported it by their attendance. He did not even mention the actors in the scene. His whole condemnation seemed to fall upon the audience. He rebuked those who already, He said, had lowered their heads in shame over the scene at the opening of the Pageant, but had not had the moral courage to leave the house.

" 'And then after a most tremendous statement concerning the terrible results which had come to New York in the way of impurity and the downfall of womanhood and manhood from witnessing such theatrical presentation, the climax of the entire astonishing scene came. Nothing like it has ever been witnessed in any theater in America.

" 'Avonarina was still kneeling at the front of the stage, her eyes glowing, her gaze fixed on Jesus as He still stood in the place where He had arisen.

" 'He now stepped into the aisle and raised His hand, and in a tone of perfect appeal commanded all who respected themselves, their children, the good name of the city, the heritage of those yet unborn, in the love of purity and honor and common decency of thought, to follow Him and leave the scene.

" 'For an instant there was not a movement. Jesus Himself was walking up the aisle alone. Then, as if by agreement, people began to rise all over the house. Even at the farthest distance, people sitting in the rear seats could be seen getting up.

" 'Row after row of men and women rose and began to stream toward the foyers. The number was increasing every moment. There were more leaving than remaining. Afterwards an estimate was made, showing that over twenty-eight hundred went out. It was a most bewildering sight, unthought of in the wildest imagining of a theater-going public. For New York has, to confess truth, presented to patrons of theatrical amusements some very questionable plays in moral standard and never before has anyone gone out to express disapproval.

" 'But a more astounding scene was enacted in the main entrance at the foot of the staircase.

" 'Manager Bardeau has been tireless in his effort to make "The Girdle of Venus" his artistic triumph of the season. He has lavished fabulous sums on costumes, stage-setting, salaries, and advertising generally. He was in the main foyer receiving the congratulations of friends after the first act and was on his way to his box when Jesus rose and stopped the Pageant. He hurried back to the foyer incensed in the extreme at this unprecedented interruption of what promised to be the beginning of a great artistic and financial success.

" 'His quickness of action is well known. Before Jesus had begun to make His appeal to the people to leave the house, Bardeau had summoned two officers. And now followed what seems to many the most convincing proof of all that this remarkable person is Jesus.

" 'Scores of people preceded Him going out, with bowed heads, passing through the exits in perfect silence, impelled as they themselves afterward said by feelings of shame and an indefinable impulse to obey the Voice.

" 'When Jesus came out, He met Manager Bardeau and the officers. Those who were near enough (and Jesus was hemmed in by the crowd going out) say Manager Bardeau used the words: "You insolent fanatic!" Then he said to the officers, "Arrest Him for disturbing the performance."

" 'Jesus glanced at Bardeau calmly and did not even

glance at the officers. He made no resistance, offered no force to anyone. He simply walked straight on. And here was the astonishing fact. The officers did not even step toward Him. They stood perfectly still and let Him walk out.

" 'It is said that Bardeau acted like a person beside himself. He raved up and down the foyer, appealing to the people to go back, but all in vain. The entire performance came to an end. Even those who remained in their seats were so excited and were so eager in discussing the matter that Bardeau himself, after consulting with his friends, declared it was impossible to continue.

" 'Now follows another phase of this whole astonishing affair. More than once it has happened in this city that a questionable dramatic performance by reformers or the pulpit has received such an advertisement from the condemnation that crowds have flocked to see it and the very denunciation of it has been the means of its larger patronage. But Manager Bardeau cannot console himself with any such expectation in this case.

" 'The perfectly terrible and scathing picture of the depraved character of the performance that Jesus uttered has put "The Girdle of Venus" as a production outside even the lowest patronage of the high life of this town. The pulpit and church generally are also tremendously aroused by Jesus' action. Public sentiment is growing stronger every hour. The recent revelations in regard to the social evil by the Expert commission has also emphasized the close connection between sexual debaucheries in New York and suggestive plays like "The Girdle of Venus." The public is clamoring for more decency and a censorship of the drama.

" 'Jesus seems to have seized the psychological moment for His action, and the people are with Him. Even Bardeau has had sense enough not to follow up his fiasco of last night and issue a warrant for Jesus' arrest. Even he realizes something of Jesus' fast increasing hold on the people.

" 'Besides all this, another event has been added to the series which has reduced Manager Bardeau to despair. Avonarina, with her passionate temperament roused to anger by the unexpected interruption of her triumph, has canceled her contract and declares no inducement will prevail on her or her company to appear at the opera house again. She will not subject herself or her people, she says, to the fanatical insults of those who claim to be the moral arbiters of artistic productions. So she is packing up her properties preparatory to a hasty and final exit from the city, leaving Manager Bardeau to face deep failure and heavy loss. Needless to say, he is in despair and is loud in his verbal expressions of hatred for Jesus and all He represents.

" 'It is practically impossible to explain to the people of this Republic who live outside of New York, the exact state in this city of public feeling which surges about the person of Jesus. Nothing else is talked of. Men and women of all classes are discussing His action, His sermons, Himself. The newspapers are bewildered in their attempt to narrate the daily events that follow His course. Scores of newspapermen have become enthusiastic disciples. A movement is on foot already to establish a daily owned and controlled by Christian men and women which shall be the organ of universal Christianity. Such a paper, it must be acknowledged, is perfectly feasible and under the impetus of the present feeling would no doubt receive large support over the entire country.

" 'The ministers and churches all over the city are rejoicing and full of hope. Jesus, according to His regular custom, is preaching in some pulpit every Sunday and holding conferences with influential leaders of all denominations. His appeal for church federation is irresistible. When once this union is effected, the saloon and vice will meet their ultimate disaster. New forces are being realized by the church every day and never in all its history did New York face such possibilities for a new and powerful redemptive change.

" 'An attempt was made last night to locate Jesus after He left the opera house. It is said this morning that He is spending much time in the ghetto. Several persons report they have seen Him east of Lenox Avenue in Harlem and several others tell of seeing Him in the Bronx and at Brownsville in Brooklyn.

" 'Over this city at present there seems to brood a spirit of mystery and power. What will come of it all? Who can tell? Society is deeply stirred. People's hearts are full of questions not yet answered. The Man moves among others apparently like others, for the most part, an average common man. At a little meeting yesterday where He was counseling with a feeble church, people said He joined in the simple lunch prepared by the young people of the Endeavour Society as if He were one of them and laughed and showed plain human humor that made Him seem like one of their own number.

" 'And yet last night He revealed certain traits that no

one can deny make Him a most extraordinary character.

" 'The very air is seemingly alive with hints of His presence and influence. He is actually among humanity living their common life and helping them to make new history. It is not the same city it was before He came. And on every lip, businessmen, newspaper editors, laborers, society people, foreigners, street car men, drivers of trucks, the heavy-hearted and the exultant, rich and poor, the ignorant and the learned, from all comes the same daily and hourly exclamation, "Jesus is here!" The future has many startling and wonderful possibilities. Who can foresee or foretell them?' "

Mr. Maxwell finished the reading. All of them were silent after it, another of those silences that inevitably followed the pressure of thought that Jesus' advent had brought to the world.

"I never was so proud of being a Christian before," said Stanton. "What a Lord and Master we have! What a Man to follow! I do not believe we have ever felt what sort of a person He was when He was here before."

"No," said Maxwell. "The world has never measured Him. It needs to study the Gospels, constantly asking the question—'Could I do that?' 'Could I say that?' whenever an incident is related or words put into His mouth."

"Thank God He is here!" whispered Virginia. "He will put new life into His church."

"Yes. And at the same time He will necessarily provoke much hatred and opposition. Men like this Bardeau and women like this notorious Avonarina will not submit to their ambitions and purposes being thwarted without trying to create some form of resistance. No doubt this will develop into something serious," said Rollin.

"Yes, and men like Jasper Carter are enraged at Jesus because He is a constant rebuke to their selfish purposes and methods. They will not endure His rule if they can help it."

"We saw Mr. Carter at the Wall Street gathering," Stanton spoke after a while. "His face expressed fear, hate, and a baffled look, as if he were possessed with a desire to break into the secret of Jesus' power—and a feeling of helplessness at the sight of it. I could not help pitying the man."

"Carter will never be satisfied until he has succeeded, as he told Barnes, in unmasking Jesus as a fraud. And he can never succeed. Poor fellow! Why, as Barnes says, does he not love instead of hate Him?"

"Why, indeed? Ask all the centuries the same question—all those who have crucified Him and said, 'We will not have this man to rule over us.' It is the world struggle against Deity. Why do people keep it up? He will draw everyone unto Himself at last."

At the very moment when the friends of Raymond were talking about him, Jasper Carter was still in New York, staying on there beyond the time he had at first planned to be absent, not settled in his own mind as to his reason for remaining after the editors' convention had adjourned and most of the newspapermen had left the city.

He had stayed with an old friend, Roswald Drake, a broker and financier. Drake lived with his family at the Plaza and was housed there in a suite of rooms that cost a small fortune to rent and keep up. He himself was satisfied with his regular meat and drink diet of money, but Mrs.

Drake and her daughters had greater ambitions. Drake himself, with the careless indifference of some rich men, deferred to his wife when the yielding did not break over into his own plans or disturb too seriously his monied ambitions. He had been present with Carter at the Wall Street appearance of Jesus and had discussed every phase of that meeting. Drake did not agree with Carter that Jesus was simply a skillful hypnotist with an unusual gift for influencing the mob. Drake was a great admirer of power.

"I tell you, Carter," he said, the morning after the scene at the theater, "that was great. I call that doing something. How many people could you or I persuade to leave after the first act of 'The Girdle of Venus'?"

Carter did not reply at once. He seemed to be brooding over matters. "You and I were present last night and were not persuaded to leave."

"But twenty-eight hundred went away. I tell you, Carter, that's unheard of. That's power, that is. You have to acknowledge power when you see it. I always do."

Drake took a drink of brandy, and lighting a cigar, he picked up the morning paper and quoted sentences here and there describing the scene. He and Carter were having a late breakfast together. Mrs. Drake and her daughters had not yet come in.

"It's great! Great!" Drake kept exclaiming. "I admire a man who can do things. Don't you?"

"Yes, if he does them fairly. But I call Him a fake."

"Fake! Who ever heard of a fake doing an impossible feat like that! Carter, you are prejudiced. Why, man, the whole city is coming to believe in Him. The *Times, Tribune, World,* and *Sun* all agree in saying that

187

this is Jesus Christ."

"Maybe you are becoming a convert," said Carter sneeringly.

"Well, hardly!" Drake laughed. "After hearing about what I would have to do on Wall Street to be a disciple, I don't know that I am ready to renounce all the good things of life as they say Clay Ross has done. They say he is actually living in the East Side, making artificial flowers at a cent a wreath. Think of Clay Ross making artificial flower wreaths and eating garlic and spaghetti with a bunch of dirty dagoes on Moore Street! If that is what it means to be a disciple, excuse me. At the same time I admire Him immensely."

"Who? Clay Ross?"

"No. He's a fool. I mean the—Person. Seeing you feel hurt to have Him spoken of as Jesus, I'll use the word Person with a capital P."

"I don't care what you call Him," said Carter shortly. "All this gush in the newspapers will fade out after a little. And He will be labeled what He is, the prince of fakes."

"You knew Him when He was in Raymond, Carter. You must have found Him out. Why don't you expose Him? As a newspaperman you owe it to the profession."

Carter turned red. "He wasn't in Raymond over two weeks. Not long enough to do anything."

"Didn't He quell a mob or something?"

"Just strong personal magnetism."

"Power, I call it," Drake chuckled. He seemed to enjoy Carter's unreasoning dislike. "How does it happen none of you editor fellows can get a photograph of this person?"

Carter was silent.

"I call that power, all right," Drake persisted. "If it's a trick, it's one you newspaper fellows don't know."

"It's a trick, all right."

"What's the harm calling it a miracle?"

"In this age?"

"What has the age to do with it?"

The same question Barnes had put to Carter.

"It's an age of science and progress, not of superstition and fairy tales."

"And yet in an age of science and progress not a single newspaper has yet got a scientific photographic picture of this person you call a fake."

"It's a trick, I tell you!" said Carter angrily.

"Oh, well, as long as you can't explain it, it's as good as the thing they call a miracle, isn't it? But I'll tell you what. We will get a closer look at this Person. All mysteries vanish at ten feet. I'll invite Him to dinner here and we'll try to find Him out. We'll test Him."

"He won't come," Carter spoke after a silence.

"Won't come! They say He goes wherever He's invited. And I reckon after dining with His Jews in the ghetto and the Italians in San Rafael Court, He won't object to a good dinner at the Plaza."

"How can you invite Him? You don't know Him."

"I don't have to. Besides, I can say in my note that a man He met in Raymond is here and is anxious to meet Him. Oh, He will come all right."

"I'd rather you did not mention my name."

"Too modest, eh? All right. Mrs. Drake and I will invite Him on the ground of our having read so much about Him and wishing to make His better acquaintance, and so forth. Of course, we want you here."

"I'll be here; but I doubt if He comes. And if He does, you never can tell what He may do or say. I had a talk with Him once and He—"

"Well? What did you discuss? Miracles?"

"No matter. You can be prepared for most anything. It will not be impossible for Him to insult you."

"Insult me! At my table!" Roswald Drake straightened up, took the cigar from his mouth, and exhibited real anger. "I know mighty well what to do if He descends to any such act with me."

"What will you do?" Carter asked in real curiosity.

"You'll see!" Drake said curtly. "I admire His power all right, but I don't stand for any foolishness such as He handed to Clay Ross the other day. Why He the same as told Clay that he was a thief and a murderer."

"Power, that's all. Power!" said Carter sarcastically.

"Power nothing! Just sheer interference in another man's business. No man living can interfere with my business as He interfered with Clay's."

"But Ross went with Him like a lamb. And they say he's turned over all his investments to rearrange everything on an honest basis."

"Honest basis!" Drake snorted. "What is an honest basis?"

"You ought to know," Carter said sharply.

Drake laughed as he reached out for the brandy. "Well, I do know. And as long as you are here, I don't give it away. But as soon as Mrs. Drake comes in, we'll frame up that invitation and get the Person to come this week. Don't make any other engagements. We need you here to watch Him and find out some of His secrets. I'd like mighty well myself to know how He does the camera trick."

Carter moved restlessly in his chair. "Suppose you ask Him how He does it?"

"I'm perfectly willing," said Drake coolly. "You editors are too proverbially modest and diffident about such matters."

When Mrs. Drake and her two daughters appeared, Drake brought up the proposed invitation, and Mrs. Drake at once acquiesced. She agreed with her husband that the Person would be an interesting Person to meet. Besides, as Mrs. Drake could not help saying to herself, He was evidently gaining great influence in the city. No such celebrity had been known for years. The papers were agreed in the statement He was really extraordinary. It would gratify a reasonable curiosity to have Him at their table; and other reasons were given by the daughters, as well.

Two days later Drake announced to Carter that the invitation had been accepted.

"We made it Wednesday night. I've asked Burrage and his wife and son, and Judge Crawford and Howard Rider and Mr. and Mrs. Silvester. They're old friends of Mrs. Drake and they'll help to keep up the conversation if it gets out of our depth."

Carter said nothing for a while. Then, suddenly: "What is your real object in asking—Him?"

"Well, I'll be honest with you, Carter. My real object is just nothing but sheer curiosity to get nearer to Him and learn something of His power. Power is my hobby.

According to the New York papers, there is no more powerful Person in the city right now than this one. I want to know why."

"Have you heard Him preach?"

"No, to tell the truth I haven't been into a church for years. I was saying to Mrs. Drake the other day we ought to go and hear Him next Sunday. They say He is great. Preaches in Beecher's old church next Sunday, I see."

"I heard Him at the Tabernacle Congregational last week. You remember I spoke of it," said Carter shortly.

"Yes, that roused my curiosity. If an old sinner like you can go to church once in ten years, I guess I can brace up and do the same. My curiosity is roused to find out what His power is."

"You're daft on 'power,' " Carter exclaimed.

"I expect I am," Drake laughed coarsely. "It's the only thing worth the game. That's the reason I hunt for it."

On the night when Roswald Drake and his wife "entertained" Jesus as their guest at the Plaza, Jasper Carter was present in an attitude that he himself could not have described. There was going on in him a conflict of passions. There had grown up in him a curious mingling of fear and hate and admiration for Jesus. In his own heart he did not yet know how strong all those passions had grown. He had almost stealthily gone into different religious gatherings in the city to hear Jesus speak. He had come away from each one of these meetings disturbed mentally and raging spiritually. And tonight he awaited the coming of Jesus as a guest at Roswald Drake's cynical, money-spattered table, with a doubt in his own mind, a feeling of strange uneasiness and unrest, added to a great curiosity to see and know this—Person—nearer. Just why, he could not tell himself.

But he found himself watching the door through which Jesus would enter. And when He finally appeared, Carter instinctively rose and watched with keenest interest the meeting between Him and Roswald Drake. And even he, prejudiced and bitter and cynical as he had become, could not resist the powerful impression as he saw these two face each other, that somehow he was looking at perfect sinlessness and God-like purpose face to face with brutal, physical, material selfishness represented by the man Roswald Drake and all his tribe.

A week after this memorable evening at Roswald Drake's, Jasper Carter was back in Raymond. The first person he met as he went into the *Gazette* office was Barnes.

During the entire absence of Carter in New York, Barnes had continued on the *Gazette* as Carter had requested him to remain, at least until Carter's return.

Barnes had wondered at Carter's prolonged absence and had not been able to account for it. Now as they met in the hall near Carter's office door, he was struck with the look on Carter's face. He looked much older and haggard.

"Come in," Carter had said abruptly. "I want to talk with you."

Barnes came in and Carter shut the door.

"This Jesus of yours will be the death of me yet," he said, speaking with forced roughness.

Barnes eyed him in astonishment. Then he said while his eye glowed: "Or the life of you, Mr. Carter."

"One or the other, let us hope," replied Carter wearily.

"But look here, Barnes, this thing is wearing on me. I went to New York, not to attend the editors' convention, but to unmask this prince of frauds. Instead of that—"

He paused so long that Barnes felt exceedingly awkward. At the same time a great light began to glow in his face as if he anticipated—he hardly knew what—but—could it be that Carter—

"No," said Carter at last as if answering Barnes's own unspoken question, "no, I'm not a convert—not yet"— (with a short laugh)—"but I want to tell you of the most astonishing thing I witnessed six nights ago at Roswald Drake's. You've read all about the Wall Street episode and the opera house scene and other events, but I don't believe this got into print or ever will—at least not just as it occurred, and I can't get to work again on the regular grind until I get it out of my system and get your opinion of it. Remember, I'm relating this, not as a confession that I am finally convinced you are right about this being Jesus (I don't concede it, not yet). I'm telling it because it really is the most surprising thing I ever saw and heard, and because I want to be fair, at least as fair as you ever knew me to be."

Barnes did not say anything, but his heart was beginning to hope vaguely for Carter.

"You don't know Drake? Well—it's not malice, for I've said it to his face—he is a sheer money-getter, with one hobby, if it can be called that—an admiration for what he calls 'power.'

"He invited—" Always Carter paused a little before Jesus' name. Now he said, "Jesus, as you call Him, to dinner, along with a number of men and women of the same tribe as himself. I was there, for I've been staying at Drake's while in New York.

"In the first place Drake's 'dinners' are at an unearthly hour and prolonged beyond all reason. He got the idea from some foreign prince he claims he once entertained.

"We did not sit down until after eleven o'clock. Jesus (you understand, Barnes, I call Him by your name for Him, not mine) sat at the right of the hostess and the left of Mr. Ord Burrage, Drake's partner; and I sat at Mrs. Drake's left, directly opposite Jesus.

"There had been nothing unusual about the talk or anything during the interval between Jesus' arrival and the sitting down to the table. I was simply impressed with two things. First, the perfect air of good sense in everything He said as He joined in the general conversation; and second, the complete calmness of His whole person. Drake is always crossing his legs and moving his foot up and down. As I looked over the assembled company at different times I was struck with the fact that there was not a calm person in the room among all those New Yorkers. Mrs. Silvester, the wife of the hotel proprietor, poses as a correctly cold and polished woman, but she is always fussing with her rings. There was not a person there who could be called calm, no one except—"

"Did you ever see Him when He was not calm?" Barnes asked as Carter broke off his sentence without finishing and then sat brooding over something.

"What! Oh, no! No, that's His peculiarity. None of the fool things said (and there were a lot of 'em) seemed to disturb Him. Drake can't talk anything but money and women. His wife has a little education enough to say a few things about books and pictures and call it art. Judge

Crawford has traveled and knows a good deal about New York, and Mr. Silvester is a keen one on business, so among them all the time up to eleven passed somehow, and Drake seemed to feel set up, satisfied with his distinguished guest and all that, though it seemed to me he was watching Him very carefully and I had not heard him ask the visitor about the camera, the picture business, you know. He had promised to do that some time during the evening.

"But after we had sat down at the table it seemed to me in some subtle manner the atmosphere changed. In the first place it seemed to me it would have been no more than—well—just common decency—you know, seeing the guest was a—well—religious person—like a—minister—for Drake to ask Him at least to say grace. In fact I was looking for it, but Drake is about the most irreligious man I know. He just hasn't any religion that I could ever detect. His whole life is simply saturated with money—and what he calls 'power.'

"There were five kinds of liquor offered and Drake had laid himself out on the menu and decorations. And all the time I could see he was trying to find an easy way to lead up to that question about the picture, and something in the attitude or manner of the guest seemed to make it difficult.

"Along toward the end of the 'dinner' (it was then about one A.M. or one-thirty), Drake leaned over the table and I thought I could see by his manner that he was about to ask Jesus the question, when a little accident happened.

"One of the servants, in removing a dish from the table in front of where Jesus was sitting, spilled its entire contents on His clothes. It was a spiced sauce of some kind and it ran down over His coat in a wide red stream.

"The servant, who was a young man, looked over at Mrs. Drake with a perfectly frightened expression, and then in the most abject manner began a profuse apology to Jesus.

"In all my life, Barnes, I think it is only fair to say, I never witnessed a finer exhibition of gentlemanly courtesy than your man Jesus showed to this frightened servant. The few words He spoke put the young man at his ease and made him feel as if a thing of absolutely no importance had happened.

"But Drake and his wife were furious. After the young man wiped off the stains from Jesus' clothes and from the tablecloth as best he could, Drake beckoned to him. He went around to where Drake sat and he leaned over and I saw Drake whisper to him a few words.

"The young fellow straightened up and his face was ghastly white. He stood a moment and then went out of the room and did not return.

"Mr. and Mrs. Drake were profuse in their apologies. Drake almost cursed the servant. Mrs. Drake spoke of him as a good-for-nothing boor. Drake said in answer to a question quietly put by Jesus that he had instantly discharged the young man from his service.

" 'He has been with me only a week,' Drake said. 'One of your recommends, Silvester,' he added with a short laugh.

" 'One of mine?' Silvester said, raising his eyebrows and speaking a little high.

" 'Well, Jarvis, your head man recommended him.

Said his mother or sister or someone was night stair cleaner or something in the hotel and the family was all right.'

" 'I don't know a thing about it, of course. If Jarvis recommended him, that's his business. All I know is it's a job to get competent servants nowadays. They can't be trusted, and they don't know a thing. You have to teach them everything.'

"Everyone at the table agreed to this and the talk drifted along to servants and their shortcomings.

"Then I saw Drake lean forward and I knew his question about the camera and the photographs was coming.

" 'It's a great thing to have power,' Drake began in that ponderous fashion of his. 'I've always admired it in anyone. And I know it would gratify the company— and—myself—if you could tell us the remarkable secret of the power that you possess to defy the scientific action of sunlight on a sensitized photographic plate. I'm sure it would be specially gratifying to my friend Carter here to know the secret of this power because he is a newspaperman himself. Of course I remember you have met Carter in Raymond. Indeed, we have discussed together several incidents that occurred there before your coming to the city.'

"It was not difficult to discover in this speech Drake's real reason for asking Jesus to dinner. He had a curiosity to learn the secret of Jesus' power not only for himself but as a sort of handsome item of entertainment for his friends who had been invited.

"Everyone in New York and all over the country now has heard of Jesus' remarkable defiance of photography.

It seems to be the one thing that has given Him the universal awe and respect of the yellow press. I have never yet granted that—"

Carter paused in his narrative and eyed Barnes thoughtfully. "Oh, what is the use, Barnes, of saying anything on that baffling topic. Jesus has never—"

Again he broke off his sentence abruptly and remained silent so long that Barnes, who was afire with curiosity to hear the rest of Carter's story, finally ventured to ask—

"What did Jesus say to Mr. Drake's question?"

"You will be astonished to hear what He said, as we all were," replied Carter as he continued his narrative.

SOMETHING TO THINK ABOUT

1. Does Jesus' behavior in the opera house seem consistent with His behavior in the Gospels? Why or why not?

2. Do you know anyone who, like Drake, is fascinated with Christ's power while untouched by His holiness?

CHAPTER X

The attitude of the different people at the table waiting for Jesus' answer to Drake's question was worth noting. "I have already told you how I was seated, directly opposite Him and at Mrs. Drake's left. Silvester, the hotel man, sat next to Mrs. Burrage, who was on Jesus' right, and Mrs. Silvester was on my left. Then came Judge Crawford and Mrs. Rider, his divorced sister, next to Drake.

"I could not help wondering a little how all these people regarded Jesus, if they had any real knowledge of His earthly history centuries ago. The more I thought of it on my way home, the more I seemed impressed with the feeling that they didn't know Him very well and regarded Him now as a distinguished or noted person who happened to be for a moment in the public eye.

"But no matter about that. They had all heard of the inability of the smartest newspapermen in New York to secure a photograph and their curiosity was excited for a moment at least beyond the usual limit even for a New Yorker.

"There was at least a full minute of silence following Drake's question. Then Jesus lifted His head and looked up at Drake as he sat at the upper end of the table and spoke. If I should try to express literally and exactly His words, I should fail to convey to you the exact impression it all made on us. I will only attempt to give you the general substance of it. You understand I am not quoting exactly as He spoke, and I cannot reproduce or imitate in any way His voice or His manner. All I can give you is the result.

" 'I will tell you,' He said, speaking very low and deliberately, 'the secret of My power if you will answer these questions I put to you.'

" 'I came here as your guest at your invitation and when we sat down at this table you acknowledged by no word or sign the great fact of the Heavenly Father who alone furnishes daily food. No hint of thanksgiving or humble and loving dependence of all humanity on God's bounty fell from your lips.

" 'During the evening no attempt has been made to discuss those great and eternal truths that always lie at the heart of all real life. All your conversation has been trivial and in the largest degree useless.

" 'Among the needless articles of unnecessary eatables placed before your guests, you put before them intoxicating drink, that criminal poison that for centuries has drenched the earth with crime, lust, disorder, shame, disease, and death. You offered no apology in putting this liquor before human beings who were made in the image of God to fulfill His righteous purposes.

" 'During the progress of the meal a young man, a servant who had been serving faithfully as he best knew how, made a very slight mistake, which made no vital difference to any human creature. For this, which you magnified as if it were a crime, you discharged him from your service, first calling him a name that contained every charge of imbecility and even wrong. You ordered him out of your service for this trivial accident in order to show your authority and because you felt socially more disturbed over an incident like that at your table than you have ever felt over great and tremendous acts in your so-called business life that have involved mighty actions of profoundest right and wrong.

" 'The questions I put to you, therefore, are these:

" 'Why do you, dependent as you are on your Heavenly Father, never by so much as a word or an act acknowledge Him or thank Him for His daily and hourly bounty? Why have you, made to be your brother's keeper and lover, set up such artificial barriers between yourself and these men you call "menials," that you live in two worlds apart, with no feeling of sympathy or affection, simply paying wages as if machines were doing your work? Do you realize that if all men and women at work with their hands should suddenly cease, all civilization would rush down into ruin?

" 'Why do you who have health and strength and mental soundness never exercise God-given faculties in honest labor? Your life is spent in making money out of others' weaknesses, in speculating on others' credulity. You have never used an honest stroke of muscular or mental power to bless this city or help make the world better. Your highest ambition is and has been all your life to make money, not by honest toil, but by gambling, by deceiving others as to your purposes.

" 'Why, with a great city full of needy humanity, have you never added anything to its uplift, never given to its betterment, never left your chase after money to help save others? Why have you, who boast of your admiration for "power," never really used any of it to love God and have spent your useless years in eating, drinking, and getting pleasures and money?

" 'Answer Me these questions and I will tell you the secret of My power. And yet it is so far beyond your spiritual apprehension that if I were to tell it to you, you could no more comprehend it than the clod can comprehend the sunbeam that falls upon it.'

"Barnes, I want to say to you that no words can express the tremendous way in which all this was said. There was no cheap declamation, no shouting, no vulgar denunciation. It was simply overwhelming in its restrained intensity. You must believe it was, to hear me say so, of all men, for I sat there in the attitude, I may as well confess, of a critic and an enemy.

"Well, I would give a good deal to be able to describe the effect of His remarks on Drake and his wife and the rest of the table. But I don't think it is possible. He sat there leaning forward in the attitude he had assumed when he asked the question. His face as I glanced at it now and then was ghastly; first white, then purple with amazement and rage. But he made no attempt to interrupt that calm, even flow of denunciation. Probably he couldn't. I don't know what it was, but there was something about it that was awful in its deliberate intensity."

Carter paused again and as he did not seem likely to continue for a time, Barnes eagerly said: "Did all this seem like—well—like an insolent or unpardonable thing for a guest to say at a man's table where he had been invited?"

Carter looked over at Barnes squarely. "No. I'm ready to say it didn't. It all sounded somehow as if He had a right to say it anywhere. The particular place didn't cut any figure.

"When Jesus had finished, He was standing up. I had never felt before how tall He is. He towered up with great dignity.

"Drake was moistening his lips and several times he seemed to choke for utterance. Suddenly he blurted out—

" 'I don't—intend—to answer—such questions from any—' And he stopped.

"After a painful silence, Jesus said: 'Neither will I answer your questions,' and then He bowed to Mrs. Drake and the rest of the company in a most perfect manner and walked out of the room.

"Now I realize, Barnes, how absolutely amazing and impossible all this seems. But the rest of it will seem even more so, perhaps.

"Drake had started up in his chair, and then suddenly he collapsed as if he had a stroke. He fell forward with his head and shoulders all over the dishes in front of him.

"Mrs. Drake screamed and everybody got up from the table in great confusion. When we lifted Drake up, he was foaming at the mouth and he glared around in a way that was frightful.

"Mrs. Drake did not seem much alarmed after the first few moments. She said he had had these attacks not infrequently of late. There was, however, great excitement among the guests. Drake seemed to be all right after a little, and it was then that I had an impulse to do what I did next, and I don't ask you to explain it, for I don't explain it myself, only tell it just as it happened, and you'll have to believe it, no matter how queer it may seem to be.

"I excused myself to Mrs. Drake and went out of the suite and started to take the elevator down to the office, when I seemed impelled to walk down the stairs instead. I think when I left Drake's apartments, I had a definite determination to follow Jesus and spy upon Him.

"But as I left the rooms, I think I had a spasm of self-reproach (think of that, Barnes, when you sum it all up) at the thought of spying on Him, and I simply started to walk down the hotel stairs without any definite purpose except perhaps to gain time with myself before I got out on the street.

"The Drakes have rooms on the ninth story. I had gone down four flights when I heard a murmur of voices down below me, and I detected Jesus' tone. It is so distinct from other voices that it is unmistakable.

"I went down one more flight and stopped on the turn of the landing. Near the hand rail at the corner there was a screen and a short sofa and a chair. I stepped behind this screen and waited a moment. Then I found I could hear plainly what was being said between Jesus and the person with whom He was talking.

"I remember I took out my watch and noted the time, a quarter to two. The voices came to me very distinctly where I stood concealed by the screen, and in another moment I understood that Jesus had stopped on the stairs to speak to one of the women employed in the hotel as a night worker to scrub the floors of the office and the stairs. I inquired afterward about these women and learned that they work between two and five A.M. and receive twenty-five cents an hour for the work.

"I will not venture to repeat exactly the dialogue I overheard, but only the substance of it. I missed a sentence here and there but caught most of what was said.

"Jesus was saying, 'The work is hard?'

" 'Well, sir, it is not so very hard, but I have not been very well lately. I don't mind it when I'm well. I'm thankful to get it.'

" 'You are not well enough to work tonight?'

" 'I have to whether I'm well or not.'

" 'You spoke of your children. Are they able to help?'

"There was a pause here in the conversation and I looked out around the screen. From where I stood I could see the woman, who was on her knees scrubbing the stairs while she talked. Jesus was standing at one side, two steps above her.

" 'I have a son, a good boy, but he has only just got a place with—Mr. Drake, here in the hotel. He began tonight. He has had experience in restaurants as a waiter, but I thought he would do better in a house. He will make a good servant. He's quick and honest.'

" 'Is his name Roger?'

" 'Yes. How did you know?'

" 'I have just come from Mr. Drake's. You spoke of a girl, your daughter.'

" 'I don't know where she is.' The woman spoke slowly and I could see her pause in her work, as she looked up at Jesus.

"Then occurred the most astonishing thing about this whole affair.

"Jesus said gently, 'You are not well. The work is too hard for you. I am strong. Let Me help you.'

" 'Well, sir, years ago of course there was much more of this work to do before they put in the new vacuum cleaners. But the stairs and office floors are marble and have to be washed, and I still have a lot of night work, but not so much as I used to, and so I fill out with washing at home, and the day and night work together, of course, makes it a little—'

" 'You are tired and sick. Let Me help you.'

"And then I saw Him get down on his knees, take the woman's brush and short-handled mop, and scrub the stairs, while I could see her crouch down, without even a word, and bury her head in a short shawl she had been wearing about her neck.

"Barnes, if this person you say is Jesus, really is the Son of God, as you believe, what do you think of a scene like that?"

"I should say it was just like Him," answered Barnes, while his face glowed and the tears stood in his eyes. "It is the best possible proof that He is the Son of God. Did He not once wash the disciples' feet? Did He not spend most of His life doing manual labor?"

"Yes—but it is not common to see men in evening dress scrubbing hotel stairs between two and three A.M. I have never seen such a sight before and it staggered me.

"I looked at it for a while, and then, not wanting to be caught in the somewhat embarrassing position I was in, I went back up three or four flights and then went out to the other end of the corridor and took the elevator there and got down, and out of doors.

"I have not seen Him since. News came in this morning, and of course you have it, about the tremendous gathering in Mount Calvary Hall at which Jesus stirred all New York over the white slave traffic, in the most startling series of revelations ever made.

"The people out over the country, Barnes, do not understand how New York seethes and boils with excitement since Jesus began to do His public work. It is indescribable. It must be said in justice to the facts that the churches of all denominations are a unit in their enthusiastic support of and belief in Him. There is an upheaval in social circles in New York. And it looks now as if some radical changes would occur that will be permanent.

"Among them is a complete change of definition of the police force. The new mayor accepts Jesus' definition of a police force as a life-saving missionary body and has begun the appointment already of a new type of officer, choosing for officers men and women of devout Christian character who, he says, will love people and save them.

"The whole thing got too much for me. I felt the need of coming home. Barnes, this has been a long spiel. Some of it, I know, has not sounded like me. Perhaps it isn't like me. But I felt as if I must tell it to someone, or I would simply choke.

"I went to New York to prove this Jesus of yours a fake. I didn't succeed. I wonder what I did do. Barnes, what do you think is the matter with me if I say—I believe—I am beginning to have a real—admiration—or something—for this—Jesus—of yours?"

"Thank God!" Barnes cried impulsively. "I believe you are not far from the Kingdom, Mr. Carter. Oh, why do you not give yourself to Him heart and mind? He is the Son of God!"

"I don't know. . ." Carter looked at Barnes actually with a wistful gaze as if he longed to know the secret of Barnes's happiness. "I'm not ready yet—"

He abruptly dismissed Barnes, who went out with a great heart throb of hope for Carter.

And when the door was shut, Carter stood still a moment, then he locked the door and went over to his desk, opened it, took the manuscript Jesus had left him out of a drawer, and sat down to read it over.

The man's soul was in chaos. He could not resume his regular work until he settled this matter. And in his memory as he struggled, there beat back and forth odds and ends of verses he had heard read from the Gospels when he was a boy and among them the phrases, "I know thee who thou art, the Son of God. Art thou come to torment me before my time?" "I will not have this man to rule over me—"

What! Call Him Master! Let Him control and direct his hitherto self-centered life! All the while He was talking there at Drake's table, asking Drake those tremendous questions about himself, Carter knew the same stern arraignment exactly fitted himself. Once (and he had not mentioned this to Barnes), once during his reply to Drake, Jesus had looked straight across the table at him, and Carter knew that Jesus meant to tell him by that look that practically all He was saying to Drake applied equally well to him and to every other self-centered soul at that table that night.

And the man knew down in his soul, as he pored fascinated over that marvelous dissecting revelation of himself in the manuscript Jesus had left with him, that he was guilty of all that it contained, that his life had been nothing but a self-satisfied hypocrisy, that he had existed to squeeze the orange of the world for his own gratification, that he had worshipped his paper for the power and the money it brought to him, and that he would never again be at peace in mind or body or heart until he settled the question of this mastery of the Person over his soul.

It must have been two hours later that Barnes in the reporters' room was startled by Carter's voice calling him.

"Come up. I want to see you."

Barnes rushed upstairs two steps at a time.

Carter was standing at his desk. The look on his face was inscrutable. "I'm going back to New York on Number Six."

"Going—"

"Yes. I want to tell you what I don't care others to know—I'm going to see—"

"Him?"

"Yes."

"Thank God."

"Wait! I don't yet know what for. Only—I know I've got to go. I've just got to go."

"Mr. Carter, do you want—"

"No," almost fiercely. "I don't want your company or your advice. I'm going on my own account. I don't care what comes to the paper—let it go to the devil—I—"

He turned back to his desk and picked up the manuscript, and Barnes saw him put it in his pocket. Then he turned around and eyed Barnes.

"I'll come back either a Christian—or—"

Then he strode out past Barnes and down into the

office, where he left directions to be followed during his absence.

Number Six, limited, carried Jasper Carter east, and every minute that brought him nearer that Figure of the Man in New York was filled with upheaval of a man's soul buffeted in the age-long struggle of obedience or disobedience to the rule of the divine.

The night woman on the stairs at the Plaza was deathly weary. She sat there on the stair while Jesus, all unknown to her, completed her task. The woman's body was so exhausted by illness and her mind so stunned or deadened by misfortune and trouble that not even the astonishing offer of this well-dressed man to help her could astonish her overmuch.

She had accepted His offer without a word. Dumb and exhausted, she had thrown her shawl over her head and in a moment she was in a condition half asleep, wholly worn out, while the waking vision of a wayward daughter, a drunken husband, and a dependent son haunted her troubled mind.

At the end of an uncounted period of time the woman was conscious of the living presence of this stranger again. What was He saying? Her mind feebly groped about to weave again the broken threads of memory.

What was that passing form of gracious helpfulness?

"Daughter, your task is done. Return home and rest there." And then, as He passed down the stairs by her, He had placed a hand on her head as she sat there bowed in weariness, and the touch was as light as a passing breath, and yet—

What was this renewing of her vital forces! How good life was after all! How deep were the wells of satisfaction that even yet could flow under the dry and burned-off wilderness of a broken heart! She sat up and drew the shawl back from her head.

Her mind felt wonderfully calm and her body was free from that deadly lethargy. She stood up and looked at her hands, wrinkled and rough and scarred with incessant use. They were the same, but she felt so strong, so fit to bear burdens, that she almost longed to begin her nightly task again.

But that had been all accomplished by this stranger. What manner of man was that! She began to feel a strange and bewildering awe as if something great and unexplainable had passed by. And she sat there dreaming awake until dawn reminded her of the passing time.

Then she gathered up her tools of labor and went down the stairs; and leaving the things in their accustomed place below, she made her way wondering, as she passed along through the streets just awaking now to the usual day's toil of the great city, if the new vitality she felt were the result of her sleep there upon the stairs or if, in some mysterious way, the stranger—

She went up the stairs of her tenement and pushed open the door into the little rooms that were all she knew for home. How often she had dragged herself up to that door, fear clutching her heart at the thought of what she might find there on the floor. And as she now opened the door and went in, she trembled and stepped back as if the usual terror were confronting her.

But a girl who had been sitting with her head bowed

on the bare table in the middle of the room had sprung up as the woman entered. She stood there with all her cheap, painted advertisement of her calling cruelly ghastly in the morning light, her hands clenched, and furrows down through the paint on her cheeks, furrows made by hot tears.

"Mother!" the girl cried out. "Mother, I've come back home!"

The older woman stood still. The girl walked from the table unsteadily toward her.

"Mother! Don't you hear me? I've come home to stay! I want to be good!"

And then she fell all in a heap, but before her hands could touch her mother's feet, the mother was beside her, lifting her head until it lay where once it had lain as an innocent baby, on the bosom of a forgiving mother, nearest of all earthly places to the heart of God.

There, as they sat together, the girl told her mother what had come to her.

"I was in the wine room at Castalina's with—when a person came in and sat down at a table alone. I was sitting where I could see Him better than the others. And His face, Oh, Mother, it was the face of all the sorrows of the world.

"And as He looked at me, it seemed to me I knew at once the awful sin of my life and the horrible pit into which my soul was slipping. As He looked at me it seemed to me He singled me out from all in the room as a lost soul that He had come to save. And when He rose from the table, I got up, all the rest calling to me and wondering, but I put my fingers in my ears and ran out.

"He was there at the foot of the steps, and—and—then I knew it was—Jesus. Yes, even we who have been living deeply in sin have heard of His presence in this wicked city. And when I saw Him standing there, I knew it was He. Who else in all the world could have touched my wild wayward heart!

"I kneeled at His feet, Mother, and He put His hand on my head and forgave my sins and told me to go home. Oh, how can I ever thank Him! He forgave my sins! He told me to go and sin no more. And I have come home, Mother, I have come home! And I want to be good, I want to be good! He said I might be as white as snow. Oh, Mother, you do not know how good it seems to me to be at home again and your arms around me!"

Mother and daughter mingled their hearts of love and thanksgiving as they talked together. Once the mother paused in her questions to ask—"Tell me again of His appearance."

The girl related it as well as she could.

"It must have been the same!" the mother cried. And she told of her experience with the stranger in the hotel.

"Mother, He has put His hand on your head as well as mine! Do you not feel a strange, new, joyful life such as you never knew before? It is the touch of Jesus."

"The touch of Jesus!" the mother murmured. "Oh, if only your father and Roger could feel it! Then our happiness would be complete."

"If He only knew! If He only knew! He would seek them out. Can we not find Him and beg Him to touch and save them, Mother?"

"How can we find Him in this big city? Daughter,

He is too busy and too great to look after such as us."

"Mother, no. He has looked after such as us. He said to me He came to seek and to save the lost. Lost! Such as I was! Mother, let us seek Him out for Father's and Roger's sake."

And they were so possessed with this one consuming passion, that after a hasty meal, they started out together to find Him. But they were unsuccessful. No one knew where He was. The morning papers contained exaggerated and garbled accounts of the scene at Roswald Drake's, gathered from the recitals of those who had been present.

But of His own place of abode no one knew. It was said He had none, except as friends provided Him shelter from time to time. Others said He worked at His old trade as carpenter to provide Himself with money necessary for His expenses. But mother and daughter returned to the room called home, late at night, disappointed in their search, which had lasted through the day.

They ate a little food together, sorrowfully going over the unsuccessful search; at the same time, in the heart of each stirred the new life put there by the touch of Jesus. They had not lighted the gas but sat in the dark, as if waiting for something they feared and longed for.

There was a step on the stairs and along the hall and the door was opened.

"Mother!" a voice called.

"Roger!" Mother and daughter rose.

He could not distinguish their faces in the dark.

"Roger, it is your sister Ellie, come home again!"

"Ellie!" The brother folded his arms about her and they wept together, the girl for shame and joy commingled.

"Mother," said the boy, "such wonderful news for

215

you. I have seen Jesus and He—"

"You have seen Him!" mother and daughter both cried out.

"Yes. At Mr. Drake's at the Plaza. He was a guest there last night. You know I began my work at Mr. Drake's last night and Jesus was at the table. And I had an accident and Mr. Drake discharged me—"

"Discharged you!"

"Yes. But Jesus sought me out and today He found me a new place in the home of one of His friends, a Christian man. I am to have a regular place, at forty dollars a month to begin with and more if I do my work right. Oh, Mother, it seems like a dream to me! To think that Jesus has actually touched me and helped me! I cannot make it real. Only I know I have the position. I am to begin in my new place tomorrow."

Then mother and daughter related their bewildering experiences to the young man. Again and again the three recounted all that had happened. Roger told of the scene at the table up to the time of his dismissal. Again and again he tried to explain the manner of Jesus when the accident occurred.

"I was frightened to death. It seemed to me I should faint away. But something about His voice and look and manner when He turned and looked up at me made me feel as if I had known Him all my life and worked with Him at the same table. Oh, it is wonderful!"

"It is the event of our lives," said the mother. Then as they still sat there in the darkness she added, trembling, "Oh, children, if only your father could meet Him and be healed."

216

"Father!" cried the girl. "Father! Could anyone heal him? He is too far gone!" A light seemed to shine in her face. "No! No! He healed me! And I was lost! He could save even Father, if—"

They sat together in the darkened room, murmuring prayers, waiting as if for something—they hardly knew what—until it was late, late into the night.

The noises of the street and the tenement had died down. Steps up and down the stairs and along the corridors had ceased. And still they sat there, close together, whispering, praying, longing, fearing, anticipating, awaiting—they did not know what—until it was almost morning—

Then there came up the stairs and after a short pause at the head of the landing a firm strong step that stopped in front of the door. They had all risen and stood there in the dark, holding one another by the hand as the door opened. The step came into the room and the door was shut.

"Lucy!" a quiet voice spoke. "Lucy, are you here?"

"Yes, John," the wife's voice trembling, hardly audible, spoke. "We are all here."

"All?"

"Ellie and Roger and I."

"Ellie?"

"Yes. She has come home."

"Thank God! Turn on the light, Lucy. I have great news for you!"

With trembling hands the woman lighted the one gas jet in the room. As the flame flared up, she saw her husband, caught a look of his face, and then as she was

217

about to fall—he sprang toward her and caught her in his arms.

"Saved! Lucy! Saved by the touch of Jesus! Oh thank God, children! I have seen Him and my sins are washed away!"

They all clung to him bewildered, as if he were one come out of the grave from the dead. As indeed he was. And then, sobbing and exclaiming for joy, they sat down while the father told his story.

"I have been drunk for three days. Tonight, early, I was going past the Bowery Mission and I stumbled in there and sat down on a back seat.

"Someone came and asked me to go down near the platform. When the meeting began, I was too drunk to understand anything about what was going on. I can remember hearing a lot of confused noises and singing and men were standing up and talking.

"Then I seemed to wake up from a sleep and felt as if something had happened out of the ordinary. A great mob of people poured into the room and down the aisle, crowding around a man who, when He turned around up on the platform and began to speak, looked right into my soul.

"I can't tell all I felt then. All I know is that He came down among us after a while and the people crowded around Him in a great mass, and as He passed by me He laid his hand on my head and I felt like a new man."

"The touch of Jesus! Oh Father, we have all of us felt it now! The touch of Jesus!" And the girl threw her arms about her father's neck and cried like a little child.

"Yes," said the man, while his tears fell over the face

of the once wayward lost girl. "It redeemed me. I am a new man in Him. The passion and the appetite are gone. Praise God! What a miracle! Praise God! Now we can understand what happened in the house of the paralytic when he walked home carrying his couch."

After a moment of unspeakable silent happiness, the father went on—

"When Jesus went out on the street I followed Him. It seemed to me I could never lose sight of Him again.

"I cannot tell all He said and did. Such a mass of people was never seen in New York before. He stood at one place and spoke to the multitude. I cannot recall it all. But I shall never forget how He spoke, as if all the city were listening, about the sin of those who made and sold liquor, and the sin of those who owned the daily papers and did not use their powerful influence to drive this sin out of the city. Such flaming words they were. The people crouched down while He spoke. It was like lightning striking down in between the skyscrapers.

"I kept following Him from place to place. The streets have been simply choked all night. But once when I was very near Him He turned and spoke to me and smiled.

" 'Brother,' He said, 'Brother! Go home and tell your wife and children what great thing has come to you. And then go out and save others!'

"And here I am. Let us thank God!"

The man fell on his knees, wife and daughter and son beside him, and prayer went up from lips that for weary, bitter, tear-stained years had known only curses and blasphemy.

Miracle of the ages, in that dingy tenement! There in that united family! Due to the touch of Jesus! One out of thousands in New York that night as the multitudes swayed and thronged about Him and cried out for His healing power.

Four days later Jasper Carter on Number Six was just entering the Pennsylvania Station, his soul possessed with feverish passion to confront Jesus face to face again. And when he met Jesus—what would his soul cry out?

SOMETHING TO THINK ABOUT

1. When you are doing something hard, feeling tired, do you ever look for Jesus' quiet presence with you? Have you ever felt Him give you new strength, as the woman working on the stairs did?

2. Why do you think Jesus dealt with the alcoholic in such a different way than He did with Drake when he served alcohol at his dinner?

3. Do you think Jesus' behavior in the Gospels is consistent with Sheldon's account of Jesus at Drake's dinner? Why or why not?

CHAPTER XI

Raymond was two days' ride from New York, and during the entire forty-eight hours of that journey, Jasper Carter had, with only a few hours' sleep taken out of his waking consciousness, been completely absorbed in his thought of this person who had at last become, in spite of himself, the center of his most absorbing interest.

As he drew nearer the city, he bought the latest editions of all the New York papers. It seemed to him as he looked them over that they contained little else except accounts of Jesus and His sayings and doings. The whole city was moved by His presence. Whenever He appeared and was recognized in public, the people streamed toward Him. The sudden cry of "Jesus is here!" was like a magic spell to attract the multitude.

But He was also beginning to arouse bitter criticism and hostility. The history of His denunciation of Roswald Drake and His public arraignment of the influential men of the press in their cowardly support of the liquor interests had aroused the hatred of those who in every age have shielded their wickedness and selfishness behind age-long custom and special privilege of social standing and wealth.

One editorial comment in particular struck Carter as significant of public feeling. He read it with conflicting feelings.

"There is a growing sentiment that Jesus is exciting

the popular mind dangerously by His denunciations of men of wealth. New York will not stand for inflaming utterances against property and the legal acquisition of riches. This is dangerous ground that He will do well to avoid treading over. Let Him confine Himself to acts of healing and the preaching of moral living. The attacks He is making on the press for its so-called friendliness to the liquor interests are absurd. The press does not stand for drunkenness or dissipation. But it has always upheld personal liberty and self-restraint. The only practical way to handle the liquor business in a city like New York is to license and regulate it. Any other method is chimerical and impractical. Even the ministers see this and accept it. The proof is seen in the absence of any agitation on this subject by the ministers and churches. Only once in a great while does any preacher in New York mention the saloon or talk about visionary prohibition. They understand that the saloon is here to stay, and it is useless to talk of getting rid of it. So they have wisely kept silent until Jesus has inflamed some of the leading pastors to begin a crusade against liquor, using very intemperate language against it and quoting Jesus as authority.

"The thing is growing more serious every day. It is not saying too much to say that Jesus is growing unpopular with the most influential people of New York. We do not deny Him great power. It cannot be denied that He has the ear of the masses. No one living in America can probably secure so large and enthusiastic an audience. At the same time, He is entering upon a stage in His career that will in the end put an end to His usefulness and destroy His influence. We say frankly that when He attacks the money interests of this city, He attacks its very existence. No man can say what He says and logically carry it out without endangering the very structure of society. We do not hesitate to declare the teachings of Jesus along this line as anarchistic and absolutely unsafe. If persisted in, they will ruin His cause and even result in His being driven out of the city as a public enemy.

" 'A public enemy,' " Carter murmured to himself. And into his mind trooped the images of Jesus' immeasurable acts of beneficence and His outpouring of self for the good of mankind in the short time He had been on earth.

And then his eye caught another staring headline printed in a sensational sheet.

"Jesus talks to the socialists. Liberty Hall jammed to the roof. Thousands outside. Tremendous excitement. Jesus is a disappointment. He refuses to outline a program. Lays down the general principle, 'Love God and your neighbor,' but will not go into details. Attitude is the same as when He said, 'Who made Me a divider among you?' " Then followed a long and lurid account of the scene at the meeting.

Another paper contained the following:

"Affairs for Jesus and His friends are reaching a crisis. Many of the most influential people in New York believe He made a vital mistake when He took up the cause of prohibition of the liquor business. He ought to have kept silent on that delicate subject. He has aroused some very influential people who are among the best citizens and who believe the saloon and brewery are here to stay and should be licensed and regulated wisely. Jesus has alienated these people by His too outspoken utterance. His best friends declare a crisis is approaching that will result in something very serious to His cause. A rumor on the street yesterday said Jesus was going to Washington to visit Congress and the President. No one could be found to verify this rumor.

"Meanwhile He is undoubtedly immensely popular with the masses. It is almost impossible for Him to show Himself in the daytime on any of the big streets. As soon as He is recognized, immense crowds assemble, blocking traffic and congesting travel. Jesus Himself has requested the people to gather for the hearing of His messages in the churches and halls where He is announced to speak. But no building can hold the people. Last Sunday He spoke out at the Polo Grounds. Such a crowd was never known before. He has a marvelous voice, which carries to any distance. No matter what may be said about opposition from some sources, no one can deny that every day He grows more popular with the people. They clamor for Him and drink in His teaching."

" 'And the common people heard Him gladly,' " murmured Carter as he read, calling to mind, again, a verse he knew as a boy. "And this is the man the upper classes crucified before, and—would again if—they could? And I myself have also been ready to persecute Him like Paul—"

He got out at the Thirty-Second Street exit and walked over to Fifth Avenue, thinking to go up to the Plaza and get a room there but with no plan in his search for Jesus, not certain of His place of abode, and wondering if the rumor of His going to Washington had already perhaps been corroborated by His departure.

As he was going up the steps of the Plaza, a man came out of the revolving door, and Carter recognized Drake.

Drake pulled up in surprise at the sight of Carter. "Hello! Thought you were in Raymond!"

"I was, but I've come back to the city—on—on important business. How are you?"

"I? Feel like a brown taste in the mouth all the time. Come back in and have a drink with me."

Carter observed Drake more carefully. The man was really ghastly to look at. Great puffs of fat below his eyes were bloodshot and heavy, marks of mental disquietude, and signs of irritation in his whole bearing spoke of serious conflict in the person. The sight of it all so close really shocked Carter.

"I've had a dog's time of it since that evening. Curse Him! Your friend, I mean. I grant your statement about His being a fake all right. But I'll join with any crowd to drive Him out of New York. I'll help you if that's what you have come on for. Didn't you say once that you could prove Him to be the prince of fakes? My God! I would give anything to even up that insult the other evening!"

Drake's face was so black and forbidding that Carter was actually appalled. He recoiled from him.

"Do you know where He can be found?"

"No, I don't. I heard this morning He had left town. If He doesn't go soon, I know some people that will ask Him (not too politely) to leave. But won't you come in and have a drink? I was going over to Antonelli's to get a brandy. But might as well get it here. I'd ask you to bring your stuff up to the rooms, but Mrs. Drake is not very well, been sick since that evening and—"

Carter explained that he did not expect to stay with Drake and might leave town that night. Drake did not seem to care what Carter did. As he turned to go down the avenue after an indifferent "all right," Carter noted again his physical slovenliness and general breakdown. It was so marked as to be startling.

"He looks like a man who is 'doomed,'" Carter muttered to himself. "Like so many I have known who have burned out. I said I didn't want a drink. But I don't know but I'll have to have one to forget Drake's looks when he uttered that curse on—Jesus—a 'friend of mine?'"

He went up to his room without any fixed plan except a constant purpose that he must see Jesus, and even then he had no definite or clear thought about what he would do or say if he did find Him or meet Him. The one thing that persisted in his mind was the fixed idea that he must see Him.

He sat in his room a while, doing nothing, staring out through the windows at the buildings across the avenue. Then he suddenly got up and went down into the street.

He had not gone a block before he heard a shrill newsboy's cry. He bought the first paper presented and backed up against a building to read.

The first headlines read, "Jesus has left the city: Is probably headed for Washington. Told His friends He planned to go there sometime. The churches and ministers are all tremendously encouraged by His presence here. No one can estimate the value of His stay. An air of victory always surrounded Him. Now that He has gone, the city begins to realize His wonderful power. His work was constructive and will abide. The action already begun against the saloons and selfish methods of money-getting are destined to grow into a volume of practical deeds that the city cannot measure. A great demand will be made by the ministers to secure Jesus' presence here again, and He has promised the leaders in the great World Congress that is to meet here in October that He will be present. The greatest event in the history of New York is the visit of Jesus and His words and doings while here. No one can yet estimate into what it will all grow."

Jasper Carter did not know any of the ministers in New York, but an impulse came over him as he read to go and see one and find out at first hand if Jesus had left the city and also, he said to himself, as a newspaperman, secure an unbiased opinion from the church of Jesus and His work. The entire thought of it all was, as he afterward said, interwoven into his entire restless driving of his soul into the presence and knowledge of this remarkable personality called Jesus.

He went back to the hotel and called up one of the ministers and frankly told him who he was and what he wanted. The minister cordially asked him to meet him that afternoon at the Central Y.M.C.A. Accordingly, Carter kept the appointment, and the minute the men came together, in his blunt, almost rough manner, Carter began to ask questions, which were answered with enthusiasm.

"In the first place, tell me plainly, do you have any doubt in your mind as to the reality of Jesus?"

"Doubt? As to His reality? There cannot be any. Have you ever met Him?"

"Yes, several times."

"How does He impress you?"

Carter did not answer at once, and then he said: "I don't care to answer. I wanted to get your opinion. Will you tell me how He is regarded by the ministers generally?"

"They are a unit in their belief in Him. The churches in New York were never so near a real basis of actual federation as now. The Episcopal body is ready to unite with the denominations on a basis of actual fellowship such as has not been true or possible before. The coming of Jesus has been the greatest historical event since His first coming. There has been nothing like it for centuries. New York does not begin to realize yet what astounding changes are already being made in her religious, social, and business life. They are simply revolutionary. But all of them are peaceful."

"And yet He did no mighty works."

" 'Mighty works!' What do you call 'mighty works'? If you mean spectacular acts of healing, He performed few perhaps, although I am told He used that power in many cases quietly where no news of it ever came to the general public. We shall no doubt hear of them from now on.

"But if by 'mighty works' one means the uniting of Christian disciples who have all these years been divided, if one means creating such a passion against the liquor business that it will be rubbed off the map of New York City, if one means reconstructing the basis of the commercial transactions so that greed and speculation and theft will be replaced by brotherly kindness and mutual helpfulness—why—who is there living among the sons of men who could accomplish such 'mighty works' as these?"

"Yes, granting that He has accomplished such miracles of grace—" Carter spoke with one of his old-time sneers.

"He has done it. The influence of Jesus in all these directions is irresistible. It cannot be denied nor checked."

"You are a master optimist."

"No. I believe it because I cannot help it. I am a disciple. It is marvelous to see the signs of His power all over this selfish city. When the World's Congress meets here with Jesus this coming fall, it will be the greatest gathering of Christendom this world has ever known."

Carter was silent, brooding gloomily. His deep-set eyes burned with a fever of unrest and dissatisfaction with himself.

"Meanwhile, what will He do? Can you tell me where He is? I'm a newspaperman, as I told you, but I don't put much faith in the accounts of His movements."

"There is no secrecy about them. He will go to Washington. He is probably there now. He will visit as many states as possible before the World's Congress here. He told a number of us this. I believe you will find Him in Washington this week."

Carter asked a few more questions before the men parted. And the minute he was alone, he decided on his course.

Before night he was on the Pennsylvania road, speeding toward Washington, impelled in his thought by the same persistent impulse that had driven him out of Raymond to find Jesus.

As he stepped out of the train into the new station at Washington, the first thing that caught his eyes was a headline on a paper at the newsstand. It was in letters so long and wide that he could read it a hundred feet away.

"JESUS IS HERE!"

He bought a paper and found that the account under the headline had nothing really positive to offer except a rumor that Jesus had, it was thought, been seen and recognized that afternoon on Pennsylvania Avenue. Beyond that there was not a single item of real news to locate Jesus or tell what He would do or say in the nation's capital.

The next morning the papers contained nothing anymore definite. Jesus was said to be in Washington, but no one knew where. There was a general air of expectancy all over the city as if great events were impending, but no definite knowledge of Jesus' presence that the most industrious correspondent could discover.

Like many newspapermen who lived in the middle west, Carter had never been to Washington and had never seen Congress in session. He walked up to the Capitol and went into the visitors' gallery of the House of Representatives, taking a seat directly opposite the Speaker. Over on the left he noted the seats reserved in the gallery of the members of the House, and after he had been seated ten minutes, he recognized the member from his district at home, who came down to a seat accompanied by two constituents.

If Jasper Carter had chosen on purpose to visit the House of Representatives on a day of supreme importance, he could not have selected a greater time. He had come in just in time to witness the final vote on the Interstate Commerce Bill forbidding the shipment of liquor into prohibition states.

He sat there, his old cynical habits predominating as he contemplated the historical event with a pessimism that had always seen the worst in human nature, and even now, in spite of the fact that he soon discovered this bill was going to pass by a large majority, trying to find selfish or questionable motives in the actions of the members who were about to vote for the measure.

He saw the congressman from his district, after evidently explaining some procedure to his friends, leave the members' gallery and come down into the House and take his seat, ready for the final vote. Carter knew, or thought he knew, how the member would vote. He was a man who had nearly all his life been on the side of the saloon and had, so far as Carter knew, always been for license and regulation and personal liberty. Naturally he would vote on the interstate commerce measure.

The time had come for the final vote on the bill and the reading clerk had begun to call the roll, when Carter, not knowing why, looked over to the left side gallery at the seats behind the members' gallery near where the member from his own district had been seated a few minutes before. Who was that, seated there in the crowd of eager, interested visitors?

He looked again, and—yes—it was Jesus!

He was seated there, unknown to the crowd about Him, His calm look directed down into the House, His unearthly and yet all-human attitude suggesting to Carter the invariable quiet of the Man, that unparalleled self-control and absence of the unrest that is common to humanity, He sat there, like an average man, only—different?

The clerk continued in his regular, even, loud calling of names. Carter checked them off mentally, even as he continued his fascinated gaze over to the spot where Jesus sat.

He heard the clerk call the name of the member from his district and heard the answer—"Aye." Several members near him looked over in real surprise. He himself sat bolt upright with a half-defiant look, as if challenging his right to vote as he did, but evidently his action was so great a surprise as to create a momentary sensation.

The roll call went on and was finished at last. Carter realized even before the final announcement was made by the Speaker that a great temperance measure had passed the House of Representatives by a very large majority.

His look went again to the Figure over there seated in back of the members' gallery. What a sensation it would cause if this distinguished Visitor should suddenly be discovered! Carter found himself wondering what Jesus would do. But He was not known and He continued to sit there in His usual perfectly calm manner until the House adjourned, going out with the other people who had filled the seats near Him.

And now in spite of the fact that he had come all the way from Raymond on purpose to find Jesus, Jasper Carter was in reality undecided what to do. At first he was ready to spring up and hasten out after Him. Then he asked himself as he had a score of times since leaving home, "What is it I am really after? What do I want to say to Him? What is it all about anyway?"

He was so undecided in his mind that when he finally did get up and go out of the Capitol, leaving by the front entrance, he had not even the intention of trying to hunt up Jesus immediately. He said to himself, "He is in the city. I shall have opportunity to meet Him."

But as he came down the steps, he saw the member from his district walking along toward the Office Building across the broad space between the Capitol and the new structure put up for the accommodation of the members. And by his side walked the Figure of the Man. The two were engaged in animated talk. Carter was near enough to note the characteristic pose and gesture of the congressman, and an unusual interest on his part.

An impulse seized Carter to follow at a reasonable distance behind the two. They were talking slowly, so deeply engaged in their talk as evidently to be oblivious of men whom they met. When they finally went up the steps of the Office, Carter saw them stop and then he saw Jesus bow and come down the steps.

He walked directly back toward the Capitol, going so straight past Carter that the editor had not time to avoid Him. Suddenly his old lifelong defiant spirit seemed to stir in Carter. As Jesus passed him, he held his hand up proudly and almost insolently.

Jesus looked directly at him. But what were those words so quietly but so penetratingly uttered as Jesus walked by him?

What? "Follow Me!" What! Follow Him! Be His disciple! Live by His rule of unselfishness? Bind himself to His chariot? Be His slave?

"No!"

Carter's soul stirred, shuddering and hostile.

"No!" He walked on, asking himself if Jesus had even

spoken anything, or was it a trick of his own nervousness? He cursed under his breath as he walked up the steps of the Office Building and went down the long corridor, looking for the number of the room belonging to the member from his district. When he found it and went in, he found the man alone. He knew him politically well enough to accost him by his first name.

"How are you, Ed? Thought I'd drop in and see you a minute. I don't bother you very often."

"Oh, is that you, Carter? How are you? When did you arrive? Come in."

Carter come in and took a seat by the member's desk. "I've been over to the House. Just in time to see the Interstate go through. Never expected you to vote as you did. Thought you trained with the wets. When were you converted?"

The member colored up and for the first time in his life Carter saw him embarrassed. He did not answer at once and stood silently confronting Carter, who sat there with a characteristic sneer on his lips.

"Do you want me to tell why I voted aye?"

"I'm naturally curious to know."

"Well, I don't know why."

"Good reason for a congressman to offer his constituents."

"It's the only reason they'll ever get. I had fully made up my mind to vote no, up to the time my name was called. I don't believe in this prohibition foolishness. But when my name was called, I said aye. It seemed to me someone actually whispered it to me, and I had to say it. Land sakes, Carter! Do I look like a sentimental fool to

234

be influenced in such a matter by a passing whim?"

"Not 'sentimental,' anyhow, Ed," Carter said sarcastically.

"No. Nor a fool, either. And yet—how do you account for it?"

Carter eyed him silently.

"And then on top of it all, what should happen but an unusually intelligent spectator, one of the plain people from whom I just parted out at the door, should catch up with me on my way over here and congratulate me on my vote! And I want to say he almost made me feel as if I was one of the elect. I didn't get his name or where he was from, but I wish you could have heard him, Carter. I was never so attracted by any casual stranger since I was born. What a fool I must have been not to find out who he was."

"Do you know who your 'casual stranger' is, Ed?" Carter asked, in vain trying to conceal his excitement.

"No. That's what I say. I must have been a fool not to even ask his name."

"That was Jesus you were talking with."

The member from Carter's district had been pacing the office floor. He stopped abruptly and sharply faced Carter. "What!"

"That was Jesus who was talking with you."

"Nonsense."

"I say it was. At least the person everyone calls Jesus."

"How do you know?"

"I've met Him several times in Raymond where He first appeared and I've seen Him several times in New York. Took dinner there with Him one night. Besides, He

235

passed me after He left you."

"Passed you?"

"Out there, man, on His way back to the Capitol."

"And you say that was Jesus?"

"Or what everyone calls Him," said Carter with a peculiar smile.

The congressman stood staring at Carter. At last—

"Is it the twentieth century or something else?"

"It's the twentieth century, all right," retorted Carter roughly.

"I saw in the papers this morning the rumor that He was in Washington. But what will He do here? What—"

"Yes—Congress will do well to ask what He will do with your distinguished body. There is no telling what He will do. At least, in New York He did a number of things they didn't reckon on. They tell me there won't be a saloon in New York at the end of ten years and that the rule of Wall Street is broken and all that—"

"So Jesus is here, and I have talked with Him," the congressman muttered, as if dazed at the event. "It doesn't seem possible, does it, Carter? I'd give a good deal to see Him again. There was something wonderfully fascinating about Him. Do you think He will begin His public work here soon?"

"I don't know anything about Him," Carter said shortly. He rose to go. The congressman from his district followed him to the door.

"Where did He come from? I mean, where does He stay?"

"How do I know?"

"I thought you said you knew Him."

"I have seen Him many times. He was in the gallery today."

"The gallery?"

"Right behind the members' gallery where you were sitting."

"And no one knew Him or recognized Him?"

"It seems not."

"Why didn't you—you said He passed you—Why didn't you ask Him where He was staying?"

Carter was silent, and the congressman noted his look. It was unpleasant to see a look that revealed passions Carter vainly tried to conceal.

"Find it for yourself!" he said after a while. "He makes it a practice to stay with some preacher. Of course, you're on intimate terms with some minister of the gospel!"

"Oh, of course," replied the congressman, "same as you. All the same," he muttered as Carter with a curt "good day" went out, "all the same I would give a good deal to see that—that—person again—and have a talk with Him. And to think I actually did talk—with Jesus, and didn't know it! And it is the twentieth century—"

He went back to his desk, but he was too excited to attend to any business; and after a few minutes of inactivity, he went out and, finding some members in the corridor, told them of his meeting.

At once he found the news was of absorbing interest. To his great surprise no one denied the identity of his "casual stranger," and with the greatest eagerness a gathering group thickened about him, asking questions and wondering at the probable outcome of Jesus' visit to the national capital.

Carter went back to his hotel and brooded. That chance meeting with Jesus had shaken him to his depth. All the time he was with the congressman he could hear ringing in his heart those two words of Jesus as He passed him. "Follow Me." He knew they had been spoken. It was not an illusion as he vainly tried to cheat himself into believing.

"Follow Me!" Two words had changed world history. And Carter sat there as the night darkened over Washington, fighting the battle of the ages for his old selfish life, fighting against the rule of Jesus, which he knew well would overturn the narrow, ugly, self-centered habits of fifty years and revolutionize his paper and make him a marked man in Raymond.

" 'I will not have this man rule over me,' " he repeated time and again. "I will not call Him Master." He had defied Him when He passed that afternoon. He would defy Him and His mastery always—

"Always?" How about that future he had many times heard Him mention in His sermons? What about that Judgment, he, Jasper Carter, must sometime face? Of course there was no such thing as Hell anymore, at least modern theology had seemed to ignore it; but again and again he recalled the tremendous pictures Jesus had drawn in His New York sermons of a Judgment and a dividing of people hereafter. And as for Hell, what was this he was going through now—

Meanwhile, as he struggled there for hours with the problem of his soul's relation to Jesus, marvelous events were swiftly impending in Washington.

His troubled sleep was broken early by cries of

newsboys. What was that familiar cry?

"Jesus is here! Jesus is here!"

He rose and dressed hastily and went down into the hotel office. Even at that unusual hour he found groups of men all over the lobby reading eagerly. He secured a paper and went back to his room to read it, and he was soon completely absorbed in the narrative that he read, as all newspapermen do, sifting out the reportorial exaggerations of the "story" and retaining the probable kernels of fact.

"JESUS IS HERE!"

"In confirmation to the rumor that Jesus was in the city, He suddenly, without any warning, appeared last night, and of all places! In a little prayer meeting at the Colored Emmanuel Church on K Street. There were only about a dozen people at the little church, including the pastor, Rev. Isaac Howard, and two of his deacons.

"According to the Rev. Howard, Jesus came in just after his meeting had begun and spoke and prayed. He expressed Himself as overjoyed at the progress of the Negro people in the United States and encouraged the pastor and the people to go on with their great work.

"Rev. Howard invited Jesus to go home with him, and He slept in the Rev. Howard's home last night. This morning He is to meet all the ministers at the Y.M.C.A. building. The secretary of the association was notified of His meeting at the Emmanuel Church; and before Jesus retired, he asked His consent to send out messages to all the ministers of the city to meet in conference, with Jesus this morning. Jesus eagerly and with the greatest enthusiasm welcomed such a conference, and the secretary got busy and before midnight every minister and church was notified.

"As we go to press, three A.M., it is reported that a crowd is gathering in the street in front of the Y.M.C.A. It will be difficult to manage this meeting and keep the mob out. The most intense excitement has begun to sweep though the city. Congressman Walters has come out with an astonishing story of meeting Jesus yesterday and talking with Him while going to his office from the Capitol, immediately after the passage of the Interstate Commerce Bill regulating the shipment of liquor into dry states. It is said Jesus was in the gallery of the House all the afternoon, and when the bill was passed, but that He was not recognized."

There were three or four columns more, but nothing additional that could be called "news," as Carter understood the "padding" process. He threw the paper down and brooded.

"All the world is gone after Him—" "And I, if I be lifted up—will draw all men—" "God is no respecter of persons—" What scraps of Bible verses learned when a boy swung through his memory now!

In a Negro prayer meeting! In Washington! Of all acts, wouldn't that "queer" anybody with the general public? Could even Jesus, Himself, afford to do a thing like that and retain His influence with Washington people of standing?

And yet why shouldn't He appear in a Negro prayer meeting if He wanted to? And sleep in a Negro preacher's house if invited. Was there anything wrong about a simple thing like that? Only, Carter grimly foresaw the mingled anger and disgust and scorn with which such a fact might be received.

Yet did not Jesus come to save all people? Was not His advent at the first for all the people? Was it not the most natural thing in the world for Jesus to do just what He did?

He found growing up in his heart and mind an additional feeling of admiration for this being. Grimly he was forced to acknowledge something that instinctively made him bend the knee, and he knew that nothing could prevent him from joining the mob out in front of the Y.M.C.A. building that morning to catch a glimpse of that Figure, now towering up over him, compelling his constant thought, making it impossible for him to attend to his business, whispering to him in a tone of thunder, "Follow Me!"

But would he finally yield? And if so, when and where?

Had he not missed the supreme opportunity when Jesus passed him yesterday and they had been alone? What chance would there be now that Jesus was plunged into His tremendous public work with the vast multitudes all around Him! How could He give any time to individuals? Had he not acted the fool when he passed Jesus so insolently, as if he were a stranger?

The whisper of Jesus as he went by was insistent— "Follow Me!" "Follow Me!"

Jasper Carter finally broke away from his brooding, went down to the café, ate a little, and then went, where he knew all along he would go, up to the Y.M.C.A. building as if drawn by a power he could not or dared not resist.

The minute he stepped out on the street, he knew what to expect. The stream of pedestrians was all one way, up past the White House to the Association building. When he reached the end of the narrow street on which the Association faces, he found it blocked as far as he could see. He knew from experiences in New York how it would be. And he waited in the crowd for he hardly knew what.

Three hours passed and all traffic in front of the Association was completely blocked. But at noon struggling groups of men began to come out of the building and force their way, as best they could, through the mass outside. Carter was near enough to catch the look on these men's faces and hear their comments.

He was struck with the exultant, triumphant, satisfied look the ministers bore. On nearly all faces were also marks of tears.

His old newspaper instincts seized Carter and he questioned one of the ministers who was trying, near him, to force his way out to Pennsylvania Avenue. "What was the net result of the meeting with—Jesus?"

"Net result? Who can report a meeting like that! I wish the entire city could have heard Him."

"What impression did He make?"

"Impression? It was tremendous. His subject was the Federation of Christian Forces: Its possibility and its program. It left a feeling with all of us of power. I never felt so proud of being a minister and a church member as I do at this minute. It is safe to say that is the one great feeling on the part of every minister who heard Him. I am simply hungry to get back to my work. I feel like ten

242

men. Christianity is the greatest living impulse in history. We can revolutionize Washington with it."

The minister spoke with such power that the crowd near and around him was profoundly impressed. Carter asked one more question. "Where is—He—now? What are His plans for the rest of the day?"

There was a curious silence before the minister answered. "At the close of His address He seemed exhausted. He seems a person of tremendous physical vitality, and we have all heard of the marvelous stretch of hours He can work. But He asked the friends to allow Him a few moments' rest before He came out to speak to the multitude here. You see the people will not go until He appears. He will not disappoint them. Later in the day the committee from the Ministerial Union and the Y.M.C.A. secretaries will go with Him to various points of interest in the city. He has expressed a desire to see the city. I would like to stay and hear Him speak to the crowd out here and I may have to. It looks as if I couldn't get out, but I have a funeral service to attend to and—"

"There He is!"

A cry went up from those nearest the Association doors, and Carter and the minister and everyone turned to look.

He had come out on the steps, and even at that distance Carter could detect on His face the expression of compassion for the multitudes.

Carter found himself wondering what he himself would say if he were called on suddenly to talk to a crowd like that made up of all kinds of humanity, black and white, rich, poor, senators, representatives, congressmen, day laborers, tramps, professional men, baseball players, actors, newspaper reporters, and tourists.

And as he listened, the marvel of it stole in upon him like a tide, irresistible, again convincing that this was none other than Jesus—His every look and word proclaimed it—He "spake as never man spake," He caught the multitude up in the sweep of compassion and for the time being it listened, as if it were in the very presence of Deity.

When He at last went back into the building, one of the secretaries asked the crowd not to try to get into the building to see Jesus as He was greatly in need of rest before going out again.

The crowd dispersed. Carter returned to his hotel and brooded there. Later in the day he went up to the Association building, again impelled by his vacillating impulse to find Jesus even while he had no definite purpose regarding his meeting with Him if he should have an opportunity to see Him alone.

He found, as he stepped into the lobby, an excited group of secretaries and Association members. One of the secretaries was talking. He was one of the committee who had gone with Jesus to see the city that afternoon and he was relating what had happened at the naval steel shell works.

"It was the regular day for our meeting and I had asked Jesus to talk to the men at the shops. When we went in, the men were just through with their meal. They gathered as they always do in the storeroom where the finished shells are ready for shipment.

"Just as Jesus began to speak, I noticed a group of men come into the room composed of Admiral Short and his staff and a number of expert naval engineers and gunners who are making a special investigation, you know, just now, following the action of Congress to increase naval supplies and add the new type Ralend shell.

"The whole investigating bunch stopped, as if smitten dead, right there among the men within ten feet of the platform which is near the door and I hadn't time to tell Jesus who they were. It would not have made any difference if I had.

"Well, fellows, you never heard such a tremendous sermon against war in all your life. It was simply unlike anything I ever heard. Jesus condemned the whole sentiment of war armament and made some astounding charges against the firms that supply contract material for the navy, proving that they are directly in touch with the naval powers and are regularly influencing public sentiment for war scares with other nations.

"The whole thing was simply—well—it was—just awful. I thought, of course, He was going to give the men a simple gospel talk. Instead of that, He—"

"Wasn't that a gospel talk, if He spoke against war?" another secretary asked.

"Oh, well—I suppose it was—but—out there of all places—it will queer us with the management. I doubt if we shall be allowed to hold meetings there again—

"All the time I could see Admiral Short and his crowd were ghastly with rage and fear. The recent disclosures in Germany and Great Britain over the scandals in navy supply circles have made our Department nervous, and once I saw the Admiral start forward as if to interrupt Jesus."

"He did begin to speak," said another secretary who had been present. "He said, 'Stop! You traitor!' like that. I heard it plainly."

"Yes, but Jesus turned and simply held up His hand toward him, and Admiral Short stepped back and put up his own hand suddenly as if to ward off a blow. There was something awful about it. But Jesus went calmly on. He talked so quiet that the men kept crowding up closer to hear, and when Jesus' prayer was over, they didn't move for a full minute.

"It was the most effective meeting we ever had out there. Nearly all the men were in tears. I heard man after man as Jesus shook hands with them ask Him to come again."

"When the papers come out there will be a sensation," the second secretary said. "Admiral Short and the rest were furious. We have not heard the last of it."

Carter asked about Jesus' whereabouts. One of the secretaries told him He was to be the guest of one of the ministers, but was not certain which one, as Jesus Himself did not know when He left the shops exactly where His work would take Him that night.

So Carter went back to his hotel, brooding deeper yet over the events of the day, his own course undecided, but—one thing positive—he would stay in Washington until he saw Jesus alone.

The President came out of the White House gates and turned to the right. As he stepped under the big lamp on the post, he took out his watch. It said ten minutes after midnight.

A secret service officer came down the walk a short distance away. At a signal from the President, he came up to the gate.

"I am going to walk up to the Capitol, Randall. You don't need to keep close."

The officer bowed and waited until the President had turned past the Pension Building before going on behind him.

The President went straight on up Pennsylvania Avenue, walking with head bent like a man tired physically and mentally. He turned at the soldier's monument at the opening to the Capitol grounds and, walking slowly, began to mount the steps behind the statue of Chief Justice John Marshall, the work of sculptor W. W. Story. Although the statue was put up there back of the Capitol as recent as 1884, already the pedestal showed shameful marks of decay in the stone, which had begun to crumble and crack away.

The President paused a moment to look at the sitting figure of the Chief Justice and then he went on up the many steps that led to the broad open stone esplanade at the back of the Capitol but facing the city. He came out on this stone terrace and, turning, leaned his arms on the broad casing and looked off across the head of the Chief Justice's statue at the city as it lay spread out in the night, lighted in soft and vague outline by its many electric glow-worm lights.

Just as he reached the coping, a Figure of a Man appeared at the farther end of the terrace. This Figure slowly drew near the President.

The secret service man stopped at the base of the statue within easy reaching distance from the President.

SOMETHING TO THINK ABOUT

1. What does it say about Carter that he was able to recognize Jesus' presence in the House of Representatives when no one else did?

2. Sheldon has Jesus call for unity among the churches while at the same time He speaks openly to political issues. Do you think today's churches would join together to accept Jesus' perspective on current political affairs? Why or why not?

3. Sheldon reminds us that Jesus is concerned with the large picture while at the same time He never loses sight of the individual. As Christ's representatives in the world today, do we have a hard time holding onto this same double perspective?

CHAPTER XII

A s the Figure of the Man drew nearer the President, the secret service officer started up from the statue of the Chief Justice, but a gesture from the President warned him not to leave his position. The next instant the President had turned, and with an attitude that proclaimed his complete submission in the presence of an absolute superior, he bent his head and remained standing in silence.

The secret service man had not been told not to listen and he could not help hearing the first few words before the two figures above him turned and side by side began to pace across the terrace until their forms were but dimly visible to him.

"I have come, as you requested."

And the President's agitated reply—

"I felt the need of Your—counsel—I wished to see You alone— The burdens of my office are heavy—I need You—"

"Let Me bear them with you—"

And then the voices trailed off into the night and the secret service man heard no more.

The two men paced across the terrace several times. Once or twice they stopped together and leaned against the coping, looking off across the top of the statue, off across the stretches of the city, and then they resumed their walk. Once in a while the murmur of their voices came to the secret service officer where he sat motionless at the foot of the statue.

An hour passed. And still the two figures continued to walk back and forth side by side. The secret service man still maintained his position at the foot of the statue. Far off a clock on some tower struck two. Rows of lights that had been like soft points marking building outlines had faded out. But the city still lay there below the terrace, glowing at regular intervals with the public lamps that burn all night.

At last the two figures came up to the coping above the statue and paused there. The President bowed deeply. The other Figure laid a hand upon his arm and spoke in a low earnest voice, and then—He walked slowly across the terrace and disappeared.

The President stood alone, his head bared, watching the Man until He was lost in the night. Then he slowly came down the steps to the place where the officer was waiting.

When he had come nearer, the officer could see tears on his face. The President did not attempt to conceal his emotions.

"Randall," he said, as he asked the officer, to walk by his side back to the White House. "I have had the greatest experience in my life during the last two hours. I have had an interview with—Jesus."

The secret service man was an officer, but he was also a human being. (How often the public thinks that a human being in a public uniform is something other than a man with emotions like any other.) Randall, often taken into confidence by the President, replied, "I knew it was He when He spoke. I could not help hearing the first words."

"He asked who you were as He saw you and wanted me to give you His greeting and blessing."

"He remembered me!"

"It is like Him. Who on earth is His equal! Randall, He gave me inestimable counsel. His rule of life is Godlike. Who can abide by it? But He is the most cheerful, courageous, hopeful spirit I ever met. I feel like a new man for seeing Him."

The President and his officer entered the gates of the White House at three o'clock. The city lay quiet and hushed, as if it were silent under the brooding of the Divine.

On that same night Jasper Carter could not sleep. He had come back to his room in the hotel and his evening had been spent in aimless unrest. He tried to read a book and found himself wandering in thought back to the moment when Jesus passed by him, saying, "Follow Me!" Then he found himself back there in the crowd in front of the Association Building staring again as he had so many times now during the last three months, fascinated, attracted, fighting down an impulse to surrender, to call out before the multitudes that thronged Him and cry to Him, "My Lord and my God! I will follow Thee even unto death!"

But it would mean such a surrender! It would change the current of his whole purpose in life! It would make him the wonder of all Raymond. And his soul fiercely rebelled at the call of that quiet but commanding Voice whose tones he could not silence.

He went to bed but lay wide awake thinking, thinking—

At last he rose and dressed and after a moment of indecision went down into the hotel lobby and sat staring at the late arrivals and theater parties, and then still urged by a restlessness that grew upon him, he went out on the street.

It was about half past one. He strolled aimlessly up Pennsylvania Avenue until he came to the monument at the end of the Avenue. He sat down on one of the steps there for some time and then rose and went on around the Capitol Hill and approached the building from the front.

Before he knew what he was doing he found himself going up the steps that lead to the terrace at the back. He had strolled up the avenue and the hill very slowly. When he came out on the terrace, it was half past two o'clock. He walked forward to the coping and looked out over the city.

He had been standing there a few moments when at the end of the terrace walk he heard a voice. He stood up straight, every fiber in him quivering, every sense of mind and body awaked!

That Voice! How familiar it sounded to him! He had heard it sighing over the woes of childhood and the tears of womanhood; heard it ringing in triumph over the progress of the Kingdom on earth; and he had heard it thundering in condemnation of brute human selfishness, but he had never yet heard it as it was now!

Jesus Is Here

For he realized in a moment that Jesus was over there at the end of the terrace praying! In the unfathomable earnestness and depth of His cry for the city and the people and the sinful world, His desire had finally become audible, and Carter, of all men, was alone there in the early morning hour to hear it!

Carter himself never could describe the impulse that moved him. But he had an intense desire to hear. It did not seem to him that it was wrong for him to steal slowly, imperceptibly, nearer the unseen Figure over there in the darkness, the Figure that was pleading there for—what?

He caught the words—the sentences—at last—broken cries for humanity, indescribable yearning for redemption, matchless eloquence lifted up in the most intimate companionship with the Eternal Presence—and then—after a deep stillness, he heard his own name spoken in appeal—what? What was that? Jesus was praying for him! Interceding with the Divine Love to touch his heart and transform his purposes and set his face toward his Father—

And at that, something in Jasper Carter's proud, cold, skeptical, selfish, cynical soul broke like an obstruction that had blocked the entrance of some beseeching influence that he had for long years shut out of his nature, and throwing himself down on the stone flagging, he cried out, "God be merciful to me, a sinner!"

Instantly the Voice ceased. A Figure rose from the shadows at the end of the terrace and advanced to where Jasper Carter lay. It leaned over and touched him, oh so tenderly, so graciously. And Jasper Carter struggled up to his knees and seized Jesus' hand and carried it to his lips, the first time in all his life that he had ever shown to a man any such sign of allegiance.

He felt himself lifted to his feet. And the grasp of Jesus' hand was like nothing he had ever felt. Yet even in the pale light that suffused the terrace, he noted how humanly weary He looked after His night's vigil, but the smile on His lips was the smile of Divine victory over Carter's redemption.

Together they stood there a few moments while Jesus spoke to him, moments that will be imperishable in Jasper Carter's memory; then together they went down the steps, setting their faces toward the city, the arm of Jesus about his shoulder and on his forgiven spirit the dawn of a new morn beginning to arise, a morn that would from this time forth be to him the very birthday of his eternal life.

Three days later Mr. Maxwell went up into the reporters' room at the *Gazette* office to see Barnes about some important notices. Since Barnes's conversion, he had joined the First Church and was one of Mr. Maxwell's most enthusiastic and loyal members. Maxwell rejoiced in Barnes's intelligent understanding of the church life and found a growing pleasure in his acquaintance.

"When do you expect Mr. Carter back?" Mr. Maxwell asked after the business with Barnes was finished.

"I don't know. He has been gone nearly two weeks now. I had a brief note from him saying he had left New York and was going to Washington. Hale, city editor, is in charge here, you know; he was in a few minutes ago and says the *Gazette* is going to the dogs with Carter away so much. He hasn't had a line from him since he left and—"

Barnes stopped suddenly and stared past Mr. Maxwell at the figure of Carter standing in the doorway. He had his suitcase in his hand and bore all the marks of hasty travel.

"I came in on Number Five and haven't been home. Very glad to see you, Mr. Maxwell. And you, Barnes. Can you both come up to my office a few minutes?"

Something in Carter's look made the hearts of Maxwell and Barnes beat quickly. Without a word they both followed the editor upstairs.

When they were in the room, Carter gravely shut the door, went over to his desk and sat down there, and for a few moments, he seemed to be going over a scene that made him entirely forgetful of anyone and everything else.

Then he turned toward Maxwell and Barnes, and they saw tears raining over Jasper Carter's face.

"I want you to know, you two, that I've surrendered to Him. I can't tell you all, but—I'm conquered. He is my Lord and my God. Mr. Maxwell, I want to make my public confession and be baptized and join the church next Sunday. I can hardly wait. I want all Raymond to know that I'm saved."

Maxwell and Barnes both went up to him and took his hands. They were so moved they could not speak. Maxwell's trembling lips at last managed to murmur, "My Lord, I thank Thee for this miracle!" Barnes cried like a child. He held Carter's hand in each of his while he exclaimed when he was able to control his voice: "I knew it would come to you, Mr. Carter. I had a feeling all the time that you couldn't stand out against Him. What a great thing for you and the *Gazette*."

"Yes. No one, not even myself, knows how great it will be. Only I know it must mean some very radical changes. I must see Norman as soon as possible. I've hated him so long that I am eager to get to work loving him as soon as I can. Jesus touched me. He is the King of kings and Lord of lords. I never knew what life was before. It is the mightiest thing ever happened to me. I wonder, Mr. Maxwell, if you wouldn't offer a prayer right here. Thank God."

They all kneeled. It was the first time a prayer had ever been offered up in that room. When Mr. Maxwell was through, Carter as he knelt said just like a child, "Barnes, won't you pray?"

Barnes was so moved it was some moments before he could command his voice. When he had offered an earnest prayer, there was another pause, and then Jasper Carter offered a prayer of thanksgiving, so simple and yet so profound in its revelation of a spiritual life which had, at the touch of Jesus, been awakened, that Maxwell and Barnes listened in awed emotion.

When they rose from their knees, Carter said, with a marvelous smile as he faced his friends again, "I've got to work hard and fast to make good now the rest of my life. Give me all the help you can. I'm only a child in spiritual apprehension. But I'm ready to go with Him all the way."

The following Sunday in Raymond was a day that was noted in its history, that history now so marked by so many significant events.

At the moment when Jasper Carter kneeled by the

communion table and the words were pronounced by Henry Maxwell, "My Brother, I baptize thee in the name of the Father and of the Son and of the Holy Spirit," a wave of spiritual power passed through the church so wonderful, so plainly felt by that great congregation that from many lips there trembled the words, "Jesus is here!" If He had actually come into the room at that supreme moment, the feeling that He was present could hardly have been more real.

When Jasper Carter reached his own home, after that day's great experience, he took a letter out of his pocket and read it with a feeling of deepening awe, reverence, gratitude, and wonder. It was a letter from Jesus, written from Washington, breathing Heaven's Blessing on him as he confessed his discipleship before the world and bidding him be of good cheer as he took up his cross and began his changes in the policy of his paper and throughout his entire life.

This letter he read again and again, and then put it into his pocket, and in the silence and seclusion of his own room, consecrated himself anew to the service of Him who has turned the ways of humanity upside down in all the ages and will continue to do so until He shall reign supreme over all.

Now in the days that followed Jasper Carter's conversion and the radical changes that took place in himself and his paper, tremendous events were occurring at Washington, where Jesus had continued His ministry.

He had continued to meet with His own disciples of every name, outlining plans for union of effort, encouraging in every way the thought of the great work of the church, emphasizing its historical greatness, dwelling on the fundamental facts of its accomplishments. The ministers and church workers were simply on fire with His message. They had united in an unbroken company to cleanse the city of the evils that had grown within it.

Pennsylvania Avenue, with its notorious saloons and houses of ill fame, suddenly presented itself to Jesus' disciples as a disgrace and a shame to the Republic. Great meetings were held all over the city to protest against the wrong and selfishness of centuries as represented by the liquor business. The daily papers were besieged with communications and petitions demanding that the press do its duty in a campaign against this enemy of civilization. The members of Congress in House and Senate were receiving vast numbers of letters from their constituents all over the country urging national legislation on the liquor issue so that manufacture would no longer be possible or recognized by the government as a source of revenue.

Meanwhile, at different public gatherings, Jesus had spoken boldly on great questions of plain right and wrong. All Washington will never forget the day He spoke to them about the sacred duty of the nation to keep its treaty obligations with other nations. Or when He spoke on the unity and equality of all humanity and demanded in the name of the Father of all that justice and love should mark the nation's treatment of Japanese and Chinese, of Slav and Italian and Negro.

As the days passed into weeks and the weeks into months, the interest in Jesus and His sayings and doings deepened all over the Republic and the world. As is always true, wherever He came He aroused the greatest love and the greatest hate. The Navy Leagues of the world were enraged at His bold utterances on the sinfulness of war. The manufacturers of war material actually succeeded in shutting out of some subsidized papers all reports of His utterances on the war question, and the feeling in the exclusive Army and Navy circles of Washington deepened with anger and opposition daily.

But nothing could exclude the influences of Jesus' words and acts from the great masses of the people. The throngs that poured around Him whenever He appeared on the streets and was recognized were enormous. Wherever He stayed, the house was besieged day and night with people clamoring for a sight of Him.

As the summer deepened and the date of the great World Conference of religious workers in New York drew near, there seemed to be all over the country a pervading sense of some great event, even of something that would eclipse all that so far occurred. But of its nature no one could speak. It was an unspoken awe, intangible and voiceless.

Mr. Maxwell and a company of First Church friends were together one evening at the parsonage, deeply stirred by news that had been coming to Raymond through all the months since Jesus had left New York to go to Washington. They were talking over the most prominent events and eagerly anticipating the great conference in October.

There were present at the parsonage that night Mr. and Mrs. Maxwell, Rachel and Virginia, Stanton, Rollin, Alexander Powers, Edward Norman, Jasper Carter, Barnes, Felicia and her husband, Dr. West, and Mr. Grey.

Mr. Maxwell had just finished reading a letter from one of the ministers in Washington. In it he had told of Jesus' sermon in one of the churches in which He had emphasized His overwhelming faith in the great good He had found in the world.

" 'The papers have enlarged on every dramatic incident when Jesus has denounced great evils; but they have not called attention so often to the fact that Jesus is an optimist and enthusiastic over the triumphs of His Kingdom.

" 'At the great conference that met yesterday in Washington Hall, He said in reply to questions that He rejoiced in a world which was in countless ways far better than it was two thousand years ago.

" 'In fact, the abounding note of Jesus' message is joy, and He is constantly reminding the Christians and the churches of their invincible power. One of the irresistible things about Him is His intense faith in the power of His gospel to redeem. It is overpowering in its intensity.' "

"That's what I liked about Him," said Stephen Clyde eagerly. "He never hesitated about the remedy for all the world's trouble. It was a joy to see His great faith in humanity."

"The papers," said Norman with characteristic impulsiveness, "have exaggerated and underestimated the whole attitude of Jesus. It is a source of deep thankfulness to my mind that there were no newspapers in Jesus' first earthly lifetime. If there had been, we would not have had any correct or authentic story of His words or deeds. What do you say, Jasper?"

Jasper Carter looked at his oldtime newspaper rival

with a look of affection such as grown men sometimes come to feel for each other. When it truly exists, there is nothing more beautiful in all the world.

"Edward," he said, using Norman's first name as Norman had used his, "I feel exactly as you do. One of my regrets as I look back on my own selfish newspaper career is at the false and superficial stories that came out in the *Gazette* about—Him."

Carter's voice slowed and softened at mention of the Name, the Name that always called to his memory that scene he had never told anyone, of his meeting that night on the Capitol terrace with Jesus.

"Does the letter mention Jesus' probable movements?" Stanton asked Maxwell, who had read only a few extracts.

"No. Only to say that His stay in Washington is evidently near a climax. And he adds this significant paragraph:

" 'The tremendous strain under which Jesus has lived every moment since He first appeared at Raymond is evidently telling on Him. It is something no one can measure. He has frankly told His disciples that He would have to visit other cities, and that the recent impassioned appeal to Him from the President and Cabinet of the Chinese Republic to come and bring His message to the millions over there was an appeal to which He must listen. It ought not to surprise His disciples if at any time He should disappear. He has, indeed, intimated as much to more than one of the ministers, as if anticipating their bewilderment when someday soon He would no longer be here. All we know definitely is the fact of His stay with

261

us until the great conference in New York in October.' "

There was silence as Maxwell stopped reading—one of those silences to which they were all accustomed since He came.

"Shall you go to New York for the conference?" Dr. West asked Maxwell.

"Yes. I am planning to go with Mrs. Maxwell. It is an occasion I cannot miss. And Stanton and his wife are going. And you and Rollin? Are you not?" Maxwell asked Rachel.

"Yes. Yes. We feel we must see Him again! Our hearts long to see Him."

"I want to go also," Jasper Carter spoke in the subdued voice that marked his new birth.

"It will be a great event," Maxwell said earnestly. "Perhaps the greatest in all history. I hope you can all go."

At this moment Mrs. Maxwell was called to the door by Martha. After a moment she came back into the room bringing Martha with her.

"Martha has received a letter she wants to share with us," Mrs. Maxwell said.

"It is a letter from Jesus. It came this morning," Martha said simply.

She began to read it aloud, while the company listened in awed silence. It was a letter that breathed the very spirit of the Divine, but written in words so human that every syllable of it seemed as commonly natural as Martha herself. At the close there were a few sentences remembering the Raymond friends and mentioning by name all who were present there at Mr. Maxwell's. The letter itself was a letter of good cheer and a reminder to

Martha of her own discipleship and the glad meeting she would have with Loreen in the other world.

"I wanted to share it with you," said Martha. "I shall keep it always with my New Testament He gave me." Then she went back to her work.

"Think of that!" Maxwell cried out after a long silence. "He finds time in the rush of tremendous world events to write a letter like that to a 'hired girl'! What a priceless document in the years to come!"

"Priceless indeed," murmured Stanton. "A letter from Jesus! What will be its value sometime! Martha is rich!"

There were a few lines in that letter to Martha that were startling in their simplicity and meaning. "Kindly tell the friends I am leaving Washington very soon. I have seen the new President. And I am expecting mighty things to be done for humanity under his leadership. I must visit as many other places as possible before the conference in New York."

Within the next week the news flashed all over the country that Jesus had left Washington and would visit a large number of cities during the summer months. A list of probable places was given. It was said the number of requests coming to Him beseeching His presence and His message was overwhelming. He could not possibly meet all the people. Day and night He was besieged to heal and speak and counsel with churches. He had already in His brief earthly stay given such an impetus to the churches, inspired the ministers so deeply with His practical plans for federation, that a new era had already begun for religion. People's hearts thrilled over the reforms and upheavals already under way in the cities where the multitudes swarmed. The influence and power of Jesus were seriously reckoned with by legislatures, city commissions, and by the National Congress. The liquor interests were making their last stand in the saloons of the big cities and the wealthy homes of aristocratic society leaders. But they were desperate as they tried to stem the rising tide of feeling that Jesus had begun. Newspaper proprietors and editors were beginning to note the trend of public sentiment in the business world and beginning, many of them for the first time, to break the silence of years and speak out for national prohibition. The spirit of Jesus was everywhere. Everywhere could be heard the cry spoken in hope and exultation and in prophecy of great righteousness—"Jesus is here!" "Jesus is here!"

And so the days fled by and the time for that great religious conference of all the Christians of the world drew near.

October had come. The new Liberty Hall on the site of the old Madison Square Garden Building had never before witnessed such a scene as now was presented there. From the ends of the earth they had come—the disciples of Jesus—at the call of a common longing on the part of all the churches of America to counsel together over the mighty matters of Christianity and help one another bring about the Federation of the world. And over every other thought rose constantly one feeling: Jesus is here! It dominated the heart of every eager passionate soul from India and China and Japan and Turkey, from the delegates from missionary churches in Micronesia and Ceylon and Korea and Burma and the Philippines.

The Hall was filling up with streams of people pouring in from the great entrances. Over all hung the immense oval dome, the structure that unlike the cliff dwellings that predominated in New York, made the new hall entirely unique.

A simple device was used throughout the entire building for decoration or design. It was a white cross. The platform was below the level of the audience floor and notwithstanding the tremendous size of the room, the acoustic properties were so perfect that persons farthest removed from the platform could hear any average speaker.

The prominence given the Raymond people by Jesus' appearance there first had given them a wide interest with the general public. At the request of thousands, the delegates from Raymond were asked to sit on the platform where the multitudes might see and note them. So it came to pass that stupendous day, Mr. and Mrs. Maxwell and the other Raymond friends were pointed out eagerly by the inflowing hundreds as the Hall filled.

With the Maxwells were Rachel and Rollin, Virginia and Stanton, Edward Norman and Jasper Carter side by side, Alexander Powers, Dr. West, Mr. Grey, Felicia and Stephen, and—there by Mrs. Maxwell sat Martha, humble but intensely loyal, her sins forgiven and the one unspoken longing of her heart the desire to see and hear her Master once more. She had not expected to go to the Conference, but Mr. and Mrs. Maxwell had simply taken it for granted and brought her with them, to her overflowing joy.

The day had been one of rare beauty. The night before (thousands recalled it afterward) had been so clear that the stars over the city sparkled with a wonderful light. People in big cities do not as a rule note starlight, but the effect had been so strange and compelling that it could not be forgotten.

The first session of the Conference was to be at night. The people had come so early for fear of not being able to get in, even though they were delegates, that long before six o'clock the building was crowded to its entire capacity.

There had been a regular program of speakers and topics prepared. But in the thought of all, there was in reality only one speaker and that was Jesus. The one question asked by every person once inside the Hall was, "Where is Jesus?" No one seemed to know. He had last been known to be visiting an obscure little town in the state, but the Committee on Arrangements could not give exact details. All they knew was that He had promised to be present at the Conference and they knew He would be, according to His promise.

Before seven o'clock the entire Hall was alive with people. Softly and slowly the electric star points in the dome came out, thousands of radiations suffusing the great space over which they hung.

It was noted by everyone how strangely silent all the people were. After that first eager question—"Where is Jesus?"—people went to their seats and as soon as seated they were silent. All over the vast assembly could be seen hundreds of heads bowed, faces in hands, cheeks wet with tears of emotion, on the platform no sight of groups of friends being introduced, or animated chatter of talk, but groups kneeling at their chairs, a hush over all, that smote the newly arrived delegates like a blow as they came in suddenly from the noisy clangor of the streets without.

There had been a program of music on the great organ, and a chorus of voices made up of groups of people representing all the great missions of the world. But a little before eight o'clock, the people still remaining seated in almost deathlike silence, someone (was it Martha?) upon the platform began in a clear, joyful, but astonishing calm voice to sing, "All Hail the Power of Jesus' Name." The voice sang one line alone, and then it was joined by the voices of the thousands—singing softly but clearly, a volume of melody that bore itself on wings of power up to the lighted dome and back again in triumphant glory.

The song ceased almost abruptly.

And then, although the hall was built with such massive walls that the sounds of street noises were entirely excluded, while the people sat in perfect stillness—waiting for Jesus and wondering at the emotions they did not know how to fathom—a sound seemed to be gathering without, a confused murmur at first, but gathering in volume and meaning as the people sat there waiting.

What was that! Strange cries came in from without! Those standing by the entrances received astounding word from the streets.

"A great wind has come up the harbor and is now sweeping over the city." It was the first passing of it over the roof of the dome that the people had heard, as it fell like a giant fist on its arching pride.

What was that! Those near the entrances reported the wind to be sweeping through the streets between the skyscrapers with a terrific speed. A few persons who appeared at the doorways and crowded as if terrified into the audience reported the astounding news that all street traffic had ceased. Not a car wheel turning on Fourth Avenue or Broadway. A rumor that a tidal wave was sweeping up the harbor.

And now the roar of a great unprecedented stupendous storm that seemed to be one of those exhibitions of power that Nature stores up through centuries of silent waiting was heard as plainly as if the massive walls of the Hall were paper instead of blocks of granite and marble. A cry came in from without that the great buildings downtown, the proud towers and money-making palaces of the money kings, might go down before this astounding tempest.

Mr. Maxwell had risen with all the people on the platform and calm but white-faced in the presence of what seemed a disaster of unparalleled proportions, had raised his hand and began to cry to the people to trust in the great goodness of God, when the lights in the great dome suddenly went out and total darkness fell upon the bewildered people.

Then arose the cry of panic. Not all in that room were Christians. Many hundreds had come from curiosity to see and hear. Men and women of wealth and fashion, men and women who hated and feared Him had come there that night. Those whose selfish schemes had been rebuked were there, and now their souls shrieked out in desperate fear of an unheard of, unthinkable calamity that was thrusting them into the very jaws of Death.

Cries, frenzied appeals, shouts rose. Hundreds struggled to reach the entrances. Cries came from the exits—"The Woolworth Tower! It has fallen! The whole city will be ruined!"

Vast roar of the elements! Tortured battling of the monumental buildings of the city as they groaned and swayed together! Over all, the total blackness that seemed a part of the solid mountain of wind that smote the pigmy little house of humanity as if it would strive to make of proud New York a vast heap of ruins!

And then a new cry rose, a cry of a woman's voice, Martha's, rising over all the human fear, strong and glad and free—

"Jesus is here! Jesus is here!"

Yes, there He stood in the very center of the Hall where He had been all the evening (an average man, only different?) surrounded by representatives of a dozen nationalities, one with their common humanity, identified with their sins and sorrows and joys and struggles and redemption through all the long centuries. There He stood, as Martha cried out, a glow of light about His tall calm Figure, His hand raised, a smile of majestic power on His lips, Master of the people and of the world, unafraid and Lord of all!

The people all turned toward that glowing, towering, lighted Figure. Was it a second Transfiguration?

He was speaking. And with the first word, the roar of the wind seemed to abate. What was it He said?

The eternal verities cannot be destroyed. The proud city might be laid low, but nothing can ever wipe out the human spirit. The things for people to strive after are Love and Religion and the Father God.

And then what was He pleading for, as the storm ceased and the people stood there awed beyond all measure?

Pleading for the loving union of all His disciples. Oh, that they would be one! He had waited so long through centuries of strife! Could they not, would they not come together? What were buildings and money and pleasure and power by the side of justice and right, and love and truth and purity and peace? Unite! Unite! Love one another! The cry rang over them and into their hearts like an audible flame.

And there He stood. The Light from His Figure now seemed to flow out from Him like waves of radiance. It enveloped the different races around Him. And the people now saw a wondrous thing.

He stood there stretching out both hands as in benediction. Representatives from China, Japan, Korea, Ceylon, Micronesia, Egypt, Turkey, South America, Great Britain, France, Spain, Italy, Germany, all America and Europe and Asia and Africa knelt at His feet.

And then as if with one accord, all the people fell upon their knees and bowed their heads.

The wind had ceased. A voice on the platform began again to sing "All Hail the Power of Jesus' Name." The great kneeling, bowing audience of all nations took up the song. It swelled with its volume like an angel's prayer.

They kneeled there in silence after the song—how long no one knew—but when they lifted their eyes and rose to their feet and looked up, Jesus was gone.

And back to the ends of the earth shall go the disciples

of the Master to proclaim His coming to all the people and the glad cry shall go up daily in the hearts of the sinning and suffering and needy souls all over the world—

"Jesus is here! Jesus is here!"

For is it not true, what He said: "And lo! I am with you always, even unto the end of the world!"

And He does walk the streets of the world today. And our hearts have a right to cry aloud as we do our work and bear our burdens: "Jesus is here!"

SOMETHING TO THINK ABOUT

1. What do you think is the meaning of the great wind in this chapter?

2. Why do you think Sheldon never describes Jesus directly but only through the eyes of those who saw Him?

3. Do we ever, like those at the conference, wait for Jesus' presence when all along He is already with us?

Inspirational Library

Beautiful purse/pocket-size editions of Christian classics bound in flexible leatherette. These books make thoughtful gifts for everyone on your list, including yourself!

In His Steps   The classic novel that started the WWJD movement. Charles Sheldon's story calls readers to a radical obedience to Jesus Christ.
Flexible Leatherette $4.97

When I'm on My Knees   The highly popular collection of devotional thoughts on prayer, especially for women.
Flexible Leatherette $4.97

The Bible Promise Book   Over 1,000 promises from God's Word arranged by topic. What does God promise about matters like Anger, Illness, Jealousy, Love, Money, Old Age, and Mercy? Find out in this book!
Flexible Leatherette $3.97

My Daily Prayer Journal   Each page is dated and features a Scripture verse and ample room for you to record your thoughts, prayers, and praises. One page for each day of the year.
Flexible Leatherette $4.97

Available wherever books are sold.
Or order from:

Barbour Publishing, Inc.
P.O. Box 719
Uhrichsville, OH 44683
http://www.barbourbooks.com

If you order by mail, add $2.00 to your order for shipping.
Prices subject to change without notice.